Shattered Dreams–
Lonely Choices

Shattered Dreams– Lonely Choices
Birthparents of Babies with Disabilities Talk About Adoption

Joanne Finnegan

FOREWORD BY
W. Carl Cooley, M.D.

Bergin & Garvey
WESTPORT, CONNECTICUT • LONDON

Library of Congress Cataloging-in-Publication Data

Finnegan, Joanne.
   Shattered dreams—lonely choices : birthparents of babies with
disabilities talk about adoption / Joanne Finnegan ; foreword by W.
Carl Cooley.
    p.   cm.
   Includes bibliographical references and index.
   ISBN 0-89789-286-0 (alk. paper)
   1. Adoption—United States. 2. Handicapped children—United
States. 3. Parents of handicapped children—United States—
Psychology. I. Title.
HV875.55.F55 1993
362.7'34—dc20   92-38706

British Library Cataloguing in Publication Data is available.

Library of Congress Catalog Card Number: 92-38706
ISBN: 0-89789-286-0

First published in 1993

Bergin & Garvey, 88 Post Road West, Westport, CT 06881
An imprint of Greenwood Publishing Group, Inc.

Printed in the United States of America

The paper used in this book complies with the Permanent Paper
Standard issued by the National Information Standards
Organization (Z39.48-1984).

10 9 8 7 6 5 4 3 2 1

Copyright Acknowledgments

The author and publisher gratefully acknowledge the following:

"I feel so cheated . . ." by J. W. S. printed with the author's permission.

"I feel empty . . ." and "Loving the Body" from *Life is Goodbye, Life is Hello* © 1982 by Alla Renée Bozarth, Ph.D. Published by CompCare Publishers, Minneapolis, MN. Used with permission.

"Direction" by Kay Haggart Mills reprinted from *alive now* (January/February 1988) with permission from the author.

"Speak to us of Children" from *The Prophet* by Kahlil Gibran. Copyright 1923 by Kahlil Gibran and renewed 1951 by Administrators C.T.A. of Kahlil Gibran Estate and Mary G. Gibran. Reprinted by permission of Alfred A. Knopf Inc.

"Legacy of an Adopted Child" is used by permission from the collection *Perspectives on a Grafted Tree: Thoughts for Those Touched by Adoption* edited by Patricia Irwin Johnston, copyright 1983. For further information or permission to reprint, contact the publisher, Perspectives Press, P.O. Box 90318, Indianapolis, Ind. 46290-0318.

"Our Child" by Chris Provost is used by permission of Perspectives Press (P.O. Box 90318, Indianapolis, IN 46290) from *Perspectives on a Grafted Tree: Thoughts for Those Touched by Adoption* edited by Patricia Irwin Johnston, © 1983.

"The Road Not Taken" by Robert Frost from *You Come Too: Favorite Poems for Young Readers*, © 1959 by Holt, Rinehart and Winston.

"It's time to renew our spirits . . ." by J. B. M. printed with her permission.

"All Because of You" by Angela Grafstrom printed with her permission.

Interviews with parents are printed with their permission. Some names have been changed to protect anonymity.

To the memory of my mother,

Amy Katherine Shaw Stevens
1917–1988

Her struggle with death taught me about
living with strength and courage.

and

To Brian

His birth taught me to face my
limitations and to let go.

Contents

Foreword

Life in the industrialized world during the last decades of the twentieth century has become increasingly fast-paced and complex. Previously un-dreamed-of stresses and unimagined dilemmas have become common-place. Technology has delivered the combined impact of fabulous new possibilities and their unanticipated consequences. Humankind is left scrambling to develop the moral and ethical principles needed in a rap-idly changing world. Though academicians and politicians may pon-der and reflect on these issues, families making choices are the real-life arenas in which a society's values are processed and changed.

During a similar time frame, the prospects for individuals with disabil-ities have improved dramatically. Wide acceptance of the practice of insti-tutionalization for people with disabilities has been replaced by a standard belief in the family as the most nurturing, stimulating, and ap-propriate place for all children to grow and develop. This fundamental inclusion of people with disabilities within families has expanded to in-clusion in the broader world of schools, workplaces, leisure activities, and other areas of community life. When a child is born with a disability, the assumptions are now the same as for other newborns. Families are expected to process (however painfully) the news of the disability, take their new child into their midst, cope, find a new balance, and carry on. Loving, caring for, and parenting the newborn child are viewed as insep-arable expectations of new parents. The notion that the decision not to parent a child could be made by a family as a loving and caring choice has been difficult for both lay and professional members of our culture to comprehend.

A strong and important aspect of the movement for the full valuation by society of persons with disabilities has been family empowerment. Through advocacy efforts by families and family-centered research and policymaking, families are no longer passive recipients of "expertise" but are acknowledged experts in their own rights and key stakeholders in the caregiving process. Parents' decision making on behalf of their children in the medical, developmental, and educational arenas has gained new potency and respect. Professionals and other providers of services have realized that if family issues are not made a first consideration, the benefits of treatments, interventions, and services may be seriously reduced. The one fundamental constraint on the new primacy of parental opinion is the well-being of their child. In other words, parents' choice making may not include decisions that would harm, threaten, or impair their child. A decision to withhold necessary medical care or life-sustaining nourishment from a child is not within a parent's prerogative. However, decisions that are contrary to professional advice or usual practices may not be threatening to a child's well-being. Parents may refuse certain early intervention services or choose to home-school a child with special needs and still be acting in the best interests of their child, professional advice to the contrary. The complex and enormously painful decision to choose an adoption plan instead of parenting a child with a disability must be examined in light of a family's ability to judge what may be in the best interests of the child and of the family as a whole. Since such a choice may be a loving and caring one, then the family making that choice should receive the same levels of support and respect as any other family. Furthermore, making families aware of the adoption option, providing information about the legal and logistical aspects of alternative caregiving, facilitating contact with other families who have pondered this choice, and validating the decision afterward are new challenges to professional values and practices.

In *Shattered Dreams—Lonely Choices*, Joanne Finnegan has combined the currency of her own life experience with thoughtfully organized topics that families considering an adoption plan for a child with a disability will confront or should consider. There are ample lay and professional writings about the characteristics and experiences of families *adopting* children with disabilities. Very little information has been gathered about families choosing an adoption plan for a birthchild. What information that exists has tended to focus on the consequences for a birthparent (usually the mother) after an adoption decision in the context of an "unplanned" or "unwanted" pregnancy resulting in a healthy, "typical" newborn. Similar information about families deciding not to parent a newborn with a disability born after a planned pregnancy is nonexistent. The richness and breadth of direct testimony in this book from birthparents who have chosen adoption and others who have not and from adoptive parents provides an unparalleled resource for both families and professionals.

While advocating for the right of families to consider an adoption plan and revealing that other "regular" families have pondered this choice, the overriding message of *Shattered Dreams—Lonely Choices* is one of caution and care. Getting acquainted with their child, gathering information about the true implications of his or her disability, and waiting out the initial storms of emotion are clearly needed for a decision based on parental love. Giving life to a child and having responsibility for a permanent decision are experiences that will not end with an adoption plan but will have a lifelong impact on all involved.

W. Carl Cooley, M.D.
Associate Director for Clinical Services
Dartmouth Center for Genetics and Child Development
Dartmouth-Hitchcock Medical Center
Lebanon, N.H.

Preface

When our son was born with Down syndrome my husband and I knew nothing about developmental disabilities. In those few weeks after his birth my knowledge and vocabulary expanded far more than I would ever have imagined. I would never have chosen to educate myself about disabilities or about adoption, but due to necessity, I did. I learned more in a few weeks than I ever had in a full semester college course.

One of the things I learned was the importance of language when referring to people with disabilities. At first I felt that parents of children with disabilities were reacting too defensively, but later, when I encountered my own concerns about adoption language, I began to understand their point of view. As I did more and more writing and speaking it became natural for me to put the child first and the disability second, to say "child with Down syndrome" or "children with disabilities." Throughout this book I've avoided language such as "Down syndrome child" or "disabled child" which may seem more readable, but which describes the child in terms of his or her disability.

While writing this book I studied an article by Paul K. Longmore and Dianne B. Piastro, "Unhandicapping Our Language" (provided by Criptography Incorporated, Los Angeles, CA). I also consulted parents of children with disabilities and professionals who work with both parents and children. I followed the advice of Longmore, Piastro, and the people with whom I spoke to try to avoid use of language that might be offensive. I have chosen to refer to the children in this book as "children with disabilities." I do not use the word "handicapped" unless in reference to the barriers children and people with disabilities encounter. I have chosen to follow the suggestions of Longmore and Piastro who advise against the use of euphemisms such as "physically challenged," "differently-abled," or "handi-capable." At times I use the expression "children with special needs" or refer to the disability as a "birth defect" or "condition" for the purpose of avoiding repetition.

It was late in the writing process that I met Patricia Johnston. I feel fortunate to have read her article "Speaking Positively—An Information Sheet about Adoption Language" (Indianapolis: Perspectives Press, 1991) before completing this work. I, too, had been uncomfortable with the terminology "giving up" a child, "keeping" a child, "real" parent, "natural" parent, and I especially cringed at the word "abandonment." I welcomed her suggestions to refer to parents who give birth as "birthparents," and to "keeping" as choosing to "parent" the child. The terms "giving up," "putting up for," "placing for adoption," or "relinquishing" are referred to instead as "choosing an adoption plan" or, simply, "choosing adoption." The preparation procedure for adoptive parents has commonly been called a "home study." Johnston advises that modern agencies like to refer instead to "parent preparation," an educational process whereby the parents are guided to investigate their strengths and make decisions for themselves. I refer to "home studies" in Chapter 6 within discussions about the adoptive families because that was the accepted terminology for the process when they became adoptive parents. My hope is that this book will further support positive attitudes toward adoption and that I have used language acceptable to all concerned.

I have purposely chosen to leave parent quotes as they were spoken or written. My intention is not to offend anyone but rather to value and authenticate the experiences of the families.

God's Child

You were conceived in love, in haste,
By parents who left God to decide.
Is it right, is it time?
But the time wasn't right for us.
It was meant to be for someone else.
So God placed you in my womb
To grow, to thrive, to be allowed to live.
Because I would not take the life
So miraculously achieved.
It is not my place to make that choice.

The time was not right for us.
But for you, it was time
To be born and placed in the hands
Of parents who will love you unconditionally.
You were God's gift to us
To teach us to be humble
To teach us to value human life and sacrifice.

You, my son, are teaching the world
More than you will ever learn.
You are a light to shine upon
The faces of all who see you,
But, most of all to light the hearts
Of special people who you will call your family.

You, my son, were meant to be—
Meant to be alive
To teach me to let go.

Joanne Finnegan
October 1988

Acknowledgments

A book of this sort does not happen without the effort and commitment of many people. The people who deserve the most thanks are the parents who contributed so openly and freely. The lengthy questionnaire to which they all responded awakened, for some, many painful feelings. Each of them gave more than time; they gave a piece of their soul. To respect anonymity, I can't name them all, but my deepest gratitude is extended to every one of them.

I am especially indebted to Dr. Carl Cooley. He not only deserves thanks for assuring me (again and again) I could write this book, but also for researching, advising, reading and rereading, correcting, and gently criticizing. He made himself available to help or answer questions, time and time again, even though he is extremely busy with his own work, family, and numerous other commitments. His support has been especially significant because he is both an expert in developmental disabilities and the father of a little girl who has Down syndrome.

I am grateful for Robin Blatt, who saw the need, helped me with those fretful beginning stages, and encouraged the process.

I owe thanks to Dr. Alan Guttmacher, who also encouraged the development of this book. He gave freely of his time to proofread, to provide information, and to offer support and constructive criticism.

Thanks to Janet Marchese for connecting me with so many other parents; her "free-of-charge" services are invaluable.

To Sophy Craze and Ron Chambers: Thank you for recognizing the need for this book and for patience, support, and encouragement to a fledgling author. And to the others from Greenwood Publishing Group who saw this through the final stages, especially Cathryn Lee and Catherine Lyons, thank you.

Lynn Flint became my editor late in the process. Thank you for those wonderful words of encouragement at a time when I most needed them.

Special thanks to my family—to those who may wonder if I still exist, to Sharon for helping with research, to Bob for spending more than his share of time parenting and for taking on additional household duties, and to my very special Katie for bringing hugs and "presents" while I was "attached" to my computer—thank you for letting me do what I needed to do to reach out to others and to recover from the loss of our Brian.

Many friends and colleagues in the Colchester School District offered words of support and answered questions related to their area of expertise. I thank them all and give special thanks to: Donna Levesque for connecting me with Dr. Carl Cooley (without whom this book wouldn't have happened); Teri Fitz-Gerald for encouragement, support, and the loan of a computer for my beginning efforts; Lynn Hier and Nancy Spier for caring, encouraging, listening, and proofreading; Anna Johnston for correcting grammar, structure, and punctuation; Bill Romond for his computer advice; Norman Gluckman for helping with research; and Melissa Bryan for publishing advice.

There were many people who helped us work through those early days of grief and decision making; without their help I might never have felt enough resolve to attempt the task of writing a book. I am especially grateful to Evelyn Sikorski, Linda Ready, Dr. Terry Lawrence, our kind, nonjudgmental friends and relatives, and the many supportive families, both local and long distance, especially the MacDonoughs.

To my telephone friends who reminded me of the need for this book when I got discouraged—thank you. Special thanks to Ruth, who proofread and advised at the final stages, and to Randy, who I called in times of panic.

Sue Goetschius, my new friend, offered advice and "pick-me-ups." I am especially grateful for her personal support and professional advice.

Thank you to those countless others—old friends (especially Jeanne Harrison) and new, acquaintances, or people "just doing their jobs"—who asked and cared, showed interest in my project, helped me locate yet another family, gave of their time to help me find my way through a maze of research or telephone connections, supported my efforts, and recognized the need for this book.

And, last, to a very special couple who confidently welcomed Brian into their home and hearts, who care about my family and our feelings, and who have been supportive of my need to write this book—thank you.

Introduction

In April 1988, my husband and I gave birth to a son with Down syndrome. At one time the doctors would have told us to institutionalize him, but now it was implied that we had only one choice—to take him home and love him. My husband asked about adoption. The responses from the medical personnel varied from helpful to condemning. In my state of devastation, I felt that I wouldn't be able to face friends or family if we "gave away" our baby.

We took Brian home because that seemed to be what we were expected to do. Our pediatrician put us in touch with parents raising children with Down syndrome, but we found it difficult to "buy" the rosy pictures these families painted. We had both grown up with siblings with disabilities. We had a toddler at home. We knew parenting was not the bed of roses that these parents seemed to portray.

We arranged for counseling about adoption. We kept asking to talk to others like ourselves who had considered adoption, but we were told time and time again that there were no others like us and "even if there were, they probably wouldn't want to talk about it."

I wanted desperately to help our son fit into our family, but I had grave doubts about the future implications for us as individuals and as a family. I searched and searched for information about adoption. I wanted questions answered. Do parents—good parents—"give up" babies? Do marriages survive afterwards? How do you explain to your other children? How do you explain to other people? Were we the "only" parents in the world who didn't think we could parent our baby?

I remembered reading a magazine article about a family who had adopted a child with Down syndrome. If there were families who adopted these children, then there must be parents out there somewhere who had made an adoption plan for their baby. Finally, after about five weeks of searching, I found Janet Marchese of the National Down Syndrome Adoption Exchange. She provided names of couples who had considered adoption and decided to parent their child and names of families who had chosen adoption. It didn't matter to us what their final choice had been; these were real, live people who had thought like us.

We started calling the couples to whom Janet referred us. They came from all walks of life—homemakers, laborers, teachers, doctors. More importantly, they were kind, caring people who appeared to be good parents. They had survived the scrutiny of society and made a responsible, loving choice for their child and their family. Those who had chosen to parent their child were nonjudgmental and seemed to be more accepting of their child than were the parents who painted the rosy pictures. Those who had chosen adoption were firm in the belief that they had found the right path for themselves.

During the months of agony, the weeks of tears and prayers, I kept wanting to read stories of families like mine. My telephone network served to connect me to people with answers to some of my questions, but at 2 A.M. during a sleepless night I wanted tangible sources of information. I had books and articles about raising a child with a disability but nothing about choosing an adoption plan for a child with special needs. As I talked to more and more people, I found that they too wanted something to read, a more tangible connection to others "like us." I made a vow that no other parents need go through the agony of a decision like ours thinking they are the "only ones."

With the support of a few professionals and several parents, I began to collect stories from other parents like myself. My original intent was to provide a pamphlet for parents of babies or children newly diagnosed with a disability (hereafter referred to as "new parents"). But, as I interviewed more and more parents, the need for a book became apparent. The families had so much to share. There were so many different circumstances, so many feelings, so many questions to be answered. Many parents had searched for weeks to accumulate information about special needs adoption. It was clear to me that this wealth of information needed to be gathered into one book.

Originally I had hoped for a book specifically for new parents, but the messages offered from "experienced" parents clearly expressed the need to educate professionals, friends, and family. In order to address all readers, I have written to a general audience. Messages especially for new parents are offered at the end of each chapter. I hope these "Notes to New Parents" will provide the more personal connection needed for these readers who are facing agonizing decisions. These "notes" also may serve as a resource for professionals to help them find words of advice and comfort for parents.

Since my initial connections were primarily with parents of children with Down syndrome, many of the parents quoted in this book gave birth to a child with Down syndrome. As I broadened my interviews to include parents of children with other disabilities I learned that all parents, whatever condition their child has, encounter very similar feelings when considering an adoption plan. Interestingly, in spite of the intimations that others "wouldn't want to talk about it," parents were quite willing to share their experiences. Very intimate and painful details of their lives were revealed in the lengthy questionnaires they returned to me, even though most had met me only through a brief telephone conversation. Others shared by mail, without ever talking with me. Closed wounds often were opened as stories were told in hopes of helping other new parents feel less alone.

Many parents and professionals may wonder, "Who would want to adopt a child with a disability?" To answer this question, I interviewed people who chose to adopt a child, or children, with special needs. Chapter 6 introduces four families who have made a choice to adopt. They, too, shared in hopes of helping others.

Quotes from parents who lived through the experience of choosing where their child would live are the core of this book. Candid remarks about their experiences provide a depth that I couldn't have accomplished alone. This book is not "my" book, but rather "our" book. "We" all have offered ourselves to help other families feel less alone, less isolated. Please take a moment to get to know the families whose stories will unfold as you read through the rest of this book.

Lorraine, then 34, and Warren, then 35, gave birth to a daughter with Down syndrome, Maria, in December 1988. Their son, Robert, was 2 years old at the time. They have another daughter, Erica, born in February 1990. Lorraine works at a county office of the welfare department. Warren is a full-time firefighter.

Maria was born five-and-a-half weeks early. Many medical tests were ordered. In addition to Down syndrome she had a heart defect common among children with Down syndrome. She had preliminary heart surgery at the age of 2 months, and would require more surgery to correct the heart defect at about 2 years old. As a result of the heart problems she had a difficult time breathing and eating.

Kathleen was 27 and Bob was 36 in 1989 when their daughter, Laura, was born with Down syndrome. Bob is a letter carrier and Kathleen is a clerk. They have another daughter who was 17 months old at the time of Laura's birth. A son was born one year later.

Laura was born at term weighing 8 pounds, 14 ounces. The baby had small eyes which made the doctors suspicious of Down syndrome, but because she was heavy with fat cheeks they thought she was just swollen from birth. She had no holes in her heart, no crease on her hands, and normal toes. The diagnosis of Down syndrome was confirmed two days after Laura's birth.

Lexie was 27 and Scott was 31 when Sara was born in 1986. Sara was Lexie and Scott's first child. Since her birth they have had two more children, Matthew, born in 1987, and Marrisa, born in 1990.

Sara was full term, weighing only 4 pounds with a teardrop-shaped head, a disfigured leg, one kidney, and growths coming out of her ears. The diagnosis given one week later was cri du chat, a rare condition technically termed 5p minus, a defect of the fifth chromosome.

Sara was tube-fed, needed oxygen to breathe, and was on a heart monitor because of several holes in her heart; her kidney also was not functioning properly. The parents asked to sign a form that requested "no heroic measures" but were denied because a diagnosis had not yet been made. By the time a diagnosis was confirmed, the baby had begun to thrive.

Mary Ann was 28 and Hank was 41 when their son Adam was born in March 1985. Another son, Bradley, was 3¹/₂ at the time. They now have two more children—Claire, born in 1987, and James, born in 1989. Mary Ann is a secretary by profession, homemaker by choice, and Hank is an employee of a federal agency.

Hank learned that Adam had Down syndrome shortly after he was born. Mary Ann was informed the next morning. Three days later they learned that Adam had a defective heart.

Sue, a homemaker, was 33 and Rick, a carpenter, was 36 when they gave birth to their second daughter, Nicole, in December 1987. Sue and Rick's other daughter was 3 years old at the time of Nicole's birth. A son was born in December 1990.

Nicole was one week overdue, yet relatively small in size. When she was delivered she was not breathing and required resuscitation.

There has been no diagnosis for Nicole. She is developmentally delayed in all areas—gross and fine motor, cognition, and speech. She was born with a malformed left thumb, which can be surgically corrected. She has some facial features that resemble a child with Down syndrome.

Pam and Rich were 26 and 24 when their daughter Nina was born in September 1981. Their son, Vincent, was 3 years old at the time of Nina's birth. Their other daughter, Krystina, was born in April 1985.

Nina was born at term, delivered by repeat Caesarean section. There was difficulty with the delivery. It was at this time that massive hydrocephalus was discovered. Later, she was diagnosed as having 4p minus, a genetic defect occurring in 1 birth out of every 100,000. Pam and Rich were told that she was the only baby to have both conditions.

Nina was transferred to the intensive care unit at another hospital on the day she was born. She required an IV and was tube-fed. A shunt was placed in her brain to relieve the pressure from fluid buildup. Eye surgery was performed to alleviate scarred, dry corneas.

Jan and Jeff gave birth in January 1989 to their first child, a daughter, Emily, who has Down syndrome. Jan, an occupational therapist, was 31 and Jeff, a clinical social worker, was 34 at the time of Emily's birth. A fetal ultrasound at eight months' gestation revealed fetal growth retardation, but Jan and Jeff were assured that there was "nothing to worry about." Emily was born at term with a low birth weight of 5 pounds, 5 ounces. Her heart had three holes. Surgery was required for duodenal stenosis, an intestinal blockage, four days after birth.

Lee, a technical product designer of an engineering firm, and Julie, an elementary school teacher, were unable to have a birthchild and had waited nearly three years for their adopted daughter Hollie. Both Lee and Julie were in their early 40s when Hollie was born by Caesarean section in February 1989. The birth was otherwise normal, as was her birth weight. Lee and Julie have no other children. Hollie was later diagnosed as having colic, she could not tolerate milk products, and she cried painfully until she fell asleep. She was taken to an emergency room in July because of crying three hours nonstop and was diagnosed with a kidney malfunction. Developmental skills were scattered or did not appear, but both parents, seeking every possible answer, were told everything was fine and to "stop worrying." In August 1989, Hollie was functioning with only the right side of her body when Julie and Lee signed the papers to legally become Hollie's parents. She was still not sitting at 8 months. A CAT scan revealed a condition called schizencephaly with over one-fourth of her brain tissue missing. Pediatric neurologists delivered the diagnosis and explained the magnitude of her life development (i.e., motor problems, speech problems, vision field cut, mental retardation, hypertonia).

Lauren was 29 and Michael was 37 when they gave birth to their son Adam, who has Down syndrome, in March 1988. Lauren is a homemaker and Michael owns an insurance agency. Lindsay, their daughter, was 3 when Adam was born. They have another son, Seth, born in May 1989. Lauren and Michael knew their baby was a boy, determined by ultrasound in the sixth month of pregnancy. Adam was born at term after a forty-three-hour labor. Other than needing oxygen for his color, he was physically healthy.

Rona and Max were both 35 when they gave birth to Naomi in June 1988. Both Rona and Max are medical professionals with advanced degrees. Their other children, Joseph and Hannah, were ages 4 and 1 at the time of Naomi's birth. Another son was born in May 1991.

The morning after her birth, the doctors confirmed that Naomi was born with achondroplasia, the most common dwarfing condition. Naomi was placed in the intensive care nursery because there was a risk of apnea related to the shape of her palate.

Trudy, then 27, and Richard, then 30, gave birth to a son with Down syndrome, Matthew, in September 1983. Their older son, Shawn, was 18 months old at the time. Trudy is a homemaker and Richard is a quality control supervisor in the nuclear energy field. Trudy and Richard now have three more boys—Ryan, born in 1985; Corey, born in 1987; and Brett, born in January 1990.

Matthew was born three weeks early with severe heart defects and spent about two months of his first four months of life in the hospital.

Mary, then 33, and Rick, then 37, gave birth to their son Lanier, who has Down syndrome, in August 1988. Mary has a bachelor of science in education and is a homemaker. Rick is a district sales manager with a medical company. They had three other children—McGowan, Emily, and Katy—ranging in age from 4 to 8 years when Lanier was born. Another son, Chandler, was born in September 1989.

Lanier was born four weeks early. Due to placenta deprivation he was small for his gestational age, weighing 2 pounds, 13 ounces. He was placed on a respirator and ventilator to develop his lungs and maintain life.

Kevin and Ann were 25 and 23 in 1990 when their son Michael was born with spina bifida. Their other son, Greg, was 2 at the time of Michael's birth. Kevin works at a paper mill, Ann at a drugstore.

Michael was a full-term baby. He had an open defect on the bottom 5 inches of his spine. He was also hydrocephalic, a condition common to children with spina bifida. Two hours after delivery he was taken to another hospital, where he was examined by a team of specialists. Kevin accompanied Michael on the 100-mile trip; Ann was recovering from a Caesarean delivery. The specialists advised Kevin that Michael, if he lived through the day, would require surgery to close the hole in his back and to relieve the pressure on his brain. The only definitive prognosis given was that Michael would never be able to walk since the nerves controlling his legs had not developed.

Beth, then 34, and Daniel, then 36, had two other children—Bethany, age 4, and Joel, 2½—when their identical twin girls with Down syndrome were born three months premature in July 1988. The pregnancy had not been planned. Beth and Daniel do not believe in abortion, so had chosen not to have prenatal testing.

Rebecca weighed 1 pound, 15 ounces, had multiple birth defects, and died one month later. Rachel weighed 2 pounds, 11 ounces, had a heart defect and seizures, and was septic. Beth and Dan worked at grasping all the positive aspects of having given birth to a child with Down syndrome, believing their only option was raising her at home. When Rachel was released from the hospital at the age of 3 months, they took her home.

Joanne was 37 and Bob F. was 38 when Brian was born with Down syndrome in April 1988. Joanne is a high school math teacher and Bob is an employment specialist for the state. Their daughter, Katie, was nearly 3 at the time of Brian's birth.

Brian was born four weeks before the due date and was physically healthy. Joanne and Bob had refused amniocentesis partly because Katie was healthy, partly because of their concern about risks involved, and because they both felt they could not abort so late in pregnancy. A chorionic villus sample (CVS) had been considered, but it meant traveling about six hours and the risk of miscarriage was even higher than with amniocentesis.

Barbara, a psychiatric nurse, was 35 and Donn, a computer programmer, was 33 in 1986 when they learned through high resolution ultrasound that their third child, a girl, would have Laurence-Moon-Bardet-Biedl Syndrome (LMBBS), a hereditary condition characterized by extra fingers and toes, obesity, hypogenitalism, retinitis pigmentosa, developmental delays, and sometimes mental retardation. The test had been performed because their second son, Damon, then 3 years old, also has LMBBS. There was a one-in-four risk of another baby having the same syndrome. Their other son, Nathan, was 6 at the time of the diagnosis.

Barbara was working as a counselor for teen parents in the school system while she was pregnant. She started the Laurence-Moon-Bardet-Biedl Syndrome Network in 1984 and was its director until 1987.

Eileen was 33 and Louis was 31 when they gave birth to Emily, who has Down syndrome, in March 1989. Their older daughter, Danielle, was 18 months old at the time. Eileen used to work on the stock exchange, but has stopped working to stay home with her family. Louis is a police officer and works a lot of overtime. They now have a son, Michael, born in May 1990, and another daughter, Jillian, born in May 1992.

Emily was born ten days late, weighing 7 pounds, 4 ounces. She was born blue and was rushed by ambulance to another hospital.

Cathie, 37, and Frank, 38, found out through amniocentesis on July 8, 1988, that their child due to be born in December was a girl with Down syndrome. Cathie is a divorced, single parent. After being married for twelve years and then divorced for two years, Cathie didn't feel ready to marry again. Cathie's daughters, Laura, Amanda, and Lisa, were 12, 9, and 7 at the time of Angela's birth. Frank has a son, Zach, who was 16 and lives with his mother.

Cathie has a biochemical imbalance that has caused her to be hospitalized several times. She takes antidepressants and antianxiety medication on a regular basis. Although the professionals recommended terminating the pregnancy, Cathie didn't feel she could abort and found a glimmer of hope when she heard of adoption as another choice. Angela was born in November 1988.

Randy, then 34, and Dave, then 39, gave birth to Jake in May 1988. Their daughter, Casey, was 2½ at the time. Randy is a teacher of children who are emotionally disturbed and Dave is a magazine editor. They have since had another son, David Mitchel, born in July 1989.

Jake has Down syndrome. He was born three weeks early and was physically healthy.

Note to New Parents _____

If you've just received the news that your baby or child has a disability, you're probably experiencing a whole range of emotions you've never felt before. Although it may be little consolation for the depth of pain you're feeling, we offer ourselves. We share only to help you feel less alone as you search out the right path for you. What is right for one family may not be right for another. We offer our stories as we lived through our own time of grief and as we continue to heal our lives.

I feel so cheated.
You were so perfect, my little one
the small life inside of me
my tummy still flat, I knew you were growing
the first flutter
then a kick
A boy or a girl? we wondered.
But never would you be right
the whole time you grew
from pinpoint tiny to person-sized
you were never right
never perfect
We rejoiced and planned
we raised glasses to toast and
cried tears of joy
through autumn, then winter
You kicked and stretched
my tummy swelled
But even then
you were different
even then
you didn't look like us
or think like us
Precious as you were, a life we created
you weren't the baby we waited for
The showers, the painting, the preparation
the excitement and anticipation
we waited to meet and love
the person we had already loved
and dreamed of
for months while you grew
But all the time you were different
not the normal, healthy child we prayed for
and felt sure was coming
Then you arrived
so early and so quickly
Your daddy helped me breathe
and I cried out when it hurt
and the nurse said "hold on"
"the reward is your baby"

I feel so cheated.
We were on top of the world
the baby we had created in love had finally come
you nursed so slowly
we thought you were beautiful
A daughter! At last!
But then the sadness so deep and dark

so crushing I couldn't breathe
my world stopped
All I could hear was my heart pounding
All I could see was you
not small and precious like before
but slow and defective and sad
How could we have made you?
How could we not have known?
Your daddy's eyes looked into my soul
what a tragedy we had wrought together

I feel so cheated.
No flowers, no teddy bears, no tears of joy
only sadness and disappointment
and an ache in my heart that won't go away
And you, dear daughter
my beautiful daughter
will live with a family who can love you
not better than us, just differently
Our own flesh and blood
a baby girl
you'll go home to someone else
who won't feel heartache when they hold you
and look into your eyes
who will love you without fear

who won't feel cheated.

J.W.S.   4/1/91

1

Shattered Dreams

RECEIVING "THE NEWS"

> Imagine the deepest darkest abyss seething with feelings of worthlessness, hopelessness, helplessness, anger, self-derision, irrationality. Now magnify that a thousand times and you might get close to how it really feels.
>
> Max

Nearly all people grow up with the hope that they will someday have the "perfect" family. Many people envision the typical American family—two children, a boy and a girl. Happy expectations of pregnancy are kindled by the media which presents images of these perfect families and the "perfect" baby—chubby and healthy with an award-winning smile. Fears of problems that could arise during pregnancy are usually quelled by well-meaning people. Even in childbirth classes, the discussion of the "worst" centers on the use of medication during labor or on C-sections. Parents learn to expect that all will be well and they'll leave the hospital carrying the "Gerber baby" home with them.

Parents who receive the news that their baby isn't "perfect" usually experience a whole range of emotions that they've never felt before. Thoughts a parent might have include: "Why me? I did everything right during my pregnancy." "This shouldn't be happening to me, I'm only 29 (or 23, or 31)." "What have I done wrong to deserve this?" Or as Lauren said, "My whole world stopped. There was no joy, only sadness. Where was that fine and perfect baby? My happy life was turned upside down."

Many parents feel despair, pain too acute to describe. Beth and Dan felt "as if our world had ended—shock, disbelief, total and utter despair . . . and fear . . . floods of overwhelming fear." Ann described her reaction, "I was in shock. I began to shake uncontrollably. I thought it was either a lie, or a nightmare!" Some parents feel anger. Barbara, who received the news prenatally, remembers "feeling angry at both myself for getting pregnant in the first place and at the ultrasound doctor for his advice to abort this 'deformed' fetus." Other parents feel fear, guilt, or numbness. Jeff said, "I have never before or since felt so hopeless, so crushed, just as if the future of my life had been destroyed." Mary Ann felt "I'd been given a life sentence," and Joanne described her initial feeling as one of resignation: "My worst fear of pregnancy had been realized."

Some parents feel so depressed and desperate that they wish themselves dead or even contemplate suicide. Many wish their baby dead and some even have thoughts of killing the baby. Hank, who was delivered the news before Mary Ann, relates, "I was so devastated that I came close to suffocating the baby before they told my wife." Kevin felt "like I wanted to die. I was scared and confused. This couldn't be happening to us; but it was."

It's normal for parents to feel intense grief. The expectations that accompany pregnancy include the presumption that those months of waiting will culminate in a joyous event. Warren tried to describe how ill-prepared he was for the turn of events: "I expected nothing but a normal brother or sister for our son. I've heard that saying before, 'No guarantees in life,' but I wasn't prepared for such a devastating blow, mentally or physically. But who is? Wow! Did it ever open my eyes and slam me to the ground."

The circumstances under which parents receive the news are usually far from ideal. Those who receive the news shortly after the birth of the baby are usually in strange surroundings, and often the person delivering the news is someone they don't know. Usually both parents are physically and emotionally exhausted. The mother will be suffering the aftereffects of childbirth and, sometimes, even surgery. She may be medicated or recovering from the effects of medication. Shortly after Randy and Dave were told that their newborn son had Down syndrome the doctor walked Dave out into the hall and Randy overheard the doctor telling him, "She probably won't remember much of what I've told her. Just make sure she bonds with the baby."

Many parents who receive the news at birth are presented with a rosy-pictured expectation that they will be fine, yet few parents feel "fine." Even if the news is broken gently with both parents present, most feel as if they've entered a dream world, a nightmare from which they hope to wake up, but instead they lie sleepless, stomachs churning, trying to face reality.

There is no easy way to tell parents their dream of the perfect family has been shattered. Even though parents of children with birth defects have worked to educate the medical professionals about more empathetic ways to convey this news, far too often parents relate that doctors and other professionals were "cold" when delivering the news. After a series of tests, Julie and Lee received the news that Hollie, age 9½ months, would be severely disabled: "The director of the child development department broke the news curtly and abruptly. She tossed the CAT scans on the table and said, 'This isn't the child you *thought* you had.' "

Parents who receive the news without certainty on the part of the professionals hold on to the hope that these doctors are wrong. It often takes several days for conclusive tests to be completed. This waiting time can be torture. Warren says, "It was like living in agony, praying and asking God for a miracle that this was all a mistake."

Some parents may wait months, or even years, for a diagnosis, sometimes never to get one. The anger and frustration can be devastating. Sue shares, "I don't have what it takes to kill myself, but I have wondered if I would be better off dead, so I wouldn't have to live this emotional pain day in and day out."

Prenatal Diagnosis

> I'd like to reach the women who are faced with the decision of terminating their pregnancy after amnio to let them know they have other options if termination is not a route they want to pursue. You feel like you're backed into a corner with no way out.
>
> Cathie

Parents who receive the news that their baby has a disability through the results of prenatal testing usually have feelings similar to those of parents who have given birth. Unlike parents who have already given birth, however, fantasies about the baby may be worse than the reality because the infant cannot be seen or touched. And, unlike parents who have given birth, a diagnosis made early in pregnancy allows another option—abortion. Depending on which test confirmed the diagnosis, parents may be facing very limited time restrictions for decision making.

A prenatal diagnosis often forces parents into making one of the biggest decisions of their lives, usually in a short time. Like those parents of newborns who wish their babies dead, many women who receive the news prenatally want to abort immediately. Thoughts of instant abortion are common, and abortion may very well be the best choice for some families. However, parents shouldn't feel pressured into abortion by literature or medical professionals who subtly, or sometimes blatantly, encourage abortion. The decision should be made by the *parents*. Parents who decide to abort after educating themselves about the baby's condition and exploring other options will likely be more confident that their decision is right for them.

Parents who receive the news prenatally often are presented with all the worst possible scenarios. The doctor who performed Barbara's ultrasound read from a book all of the problems associated with Laurence-Moon-Bardet-Biedl Syndrome. Barbara shares:

It's like reading about a drug in the *Physician's Desk Reference,* every possible side effect is listed, but most people don't ever experience any of them. I can't recall all of what he read, but I did know that my other child with LMBBS and other children with this syndrome whose parents I had talked with did not exhibit most of these difficulties. . . . I tried to tell him that I already had a child with LMBBS and that it wasn't as bad as the book made it sound, but he didn't seem to believe me.

The doctor didn't know Barbara at all and seemed to be deriving all of his knowledge of Laurence-Moon-Bardet-Biedl Syndrome from the book. Barbara shares, "He went on to say that 'a child born with this syndrome would be destined to live a terrible life,' advised me to get an abortion—'while there's still time,' . . . shook his head, said that he was sorry, and sent me on my way." A reputable ophthalmologist/geneticist also had warned her that a second child with LMBBS "is usually worse off than the first." The family geneticist and an obstetrician who was also a psychiatrist offered Barbara and Donn facts and helped them base their decision on these facts and their own gut feelings. Barbara says, "I continue to respect them for not trying to persuade us to make what *they* probably felt was the best decision."

Cathie, too, found the professionals to be very negative about the future of her baby. Cathie's doctors highly encouraged abortion, quoting the statistics on the health, physical, and mental problems of children with Down syndrome. She felt these doctors "painted a devastating picture" and was sure she would be giving birth to a "freak." Cathie found accurate information about Down syndrome and about adoption through her own efforts in educating herself. She warns professionals that they "shouldn't be so quick to suggest terminating pregnancy," and that they "need to have more information available, more updated materials."

Parents Talk

When the doctor told us that both of our twin girls had Down syndrome, we felt that our world had ended. . . . Our two normal daughters had "died" at that point and we felt that two "monsters" had taken their place. They looked the same, but they were suddenly strangers and the cute identical twins we envisioned taking home with us were no longer there.

Beth and Daniel

When we received the news five days after Lanier's birth, we at first felt relief because we had waited so long for the confirmation of Down syndrome. Then we were in shock for about a week and then we felt incredible pain and hurt for our son and the reality of how the extra chromosome would affect our child. Then we faced the torment of whether we could raise him and cope with the pain and fear that we undoubtedly would experience.

Rick and Mary

The ten hours after her birth were the only happy moments we shared, until we received the news, by telephone, that she might have Down syndrome. The doctors told us it was not definite because she didn't have many of the Down syndrome characteristics. We felt sick and shocked.

Warren and Lorraine

I went to see Michael while Ann was in the recovery room. That's when the doctors told me he had some serious problems and that he was going to be transferred to another hospital. I was standing beside Michael when they told me. I wanted to hold him to make him better, but I couldn't.

Kevin

It was as if we knew two different little precious individuals—the one who brought with it our dreams and the other with a life so different, so painful from the one we had envisioned for all three of us. What had an innocent child who had never touched the world done to deserve this? I couldn't and didn't go to work for a week. I just lay in bed and held my baby.

Julie

When the doctor sat down on the bed with my son in his lap, I still didn't realize that he was going to tell us that our baby had a problem. I was caught up in some kind of fairy-tale existence, ignoring all of the signs around me which now seem so obvious. As soon as I heard the words "Down syndrome," I blocked out much of the rest of the conversation. I did ask to hold my baby but as soon as the doctor placed him in my arms, I thought, "If I pick up this pillow and put it over his head it will all be over." Then I felt guilty for having that thought.

Joanne

I saw my doctor approaching me in the recovery room. Deep in my heart I knew what he was about to tell me. I saw the expression on his face and just started to cry and repeat over and over, "I knew something was wrong." My husband was not there at the time; the doctor had informed him immediately after the delivery. Rich had rushed to see Nina; peered through the glass window and fell to his knees crying. His next reaction was to request a priest. He was devastated. He initially carried this terrible burden alone. I was kept sedated after the delivery for quite some time. We were really alone from the beginning. There was no one. Not even family.

Pam

There was some quiet talk between the nurse and doctor soon after my son was born and I got very alarmed, but they insisted the baby was fine and perfect; he just needed some oxygen for his color. They gave him to me, wearing his hospital hat, and I looked at him and said, "He looks like a Down syndrome baby" and I expected the nurse to say, "They all look swollen at birth," but, instead, she said, "We suspect he is." I had never seen a Down syndrome baby before, but I had known instantly.

Lauren

We were together. The pediatrician told us that, although some tests needed to be done, it was almost certain that our baby had a dwarfing condition called achondroplasia. We had to sit down. We felt hurt, deflated, angry, crushed, robbed, empty. Has this really happened to us?

Max and Rona

I was told two days after birth, in the hospital, when I was alone. The pediatrician told me the baby might have a form of Down syndrome called mosaicism. She would look a little different in her eyes but she could have plastic surgery. She would be a "C" student, not an "A" and she could go to a regular public school with regular children. They called me back two days later on the phone and said, "Yes, she has complete Down syndrome, here is a phone number if you want to talk to someone!" Then they hung up.

Kathleen

My pediatrician called us into her office about one week after the baby's birth. She told us, rather matter-of-factly, explained the disability [cri du chat], the limitations and in the same breath . . . how she would hook us up with a social worker who would inform us of available community services. We were very sad, shocked, numb. . . . I felt as though my worst nightmare had come true.

Lexie

The pediatrician told me the next morning. . . . I immediately wished the baby would die. When the pediatrician told me the baby had "a problem" I felt that he meant a physical problem such as a heart defect or blindness and that we would be able to deal with it. Mental retardation was not, for us, a manageable problem, or one we could deal with.

Mary Ann

I'll never forget that day. As I was lying on the exam table awaiting the second ultrasound, I was feeling pretty good. But as the doctor zeroed in on one of my baby's hands, he started to count, "1, 2, 3, 4, 5 . . . 6!" Then he went down to the feet and counted the toes on one foot—"1, 2, 3, 4, 5 . . . 6!" I was in shock.

. . . I sat down in his office and he said the obvious . . . since I already had one child with a genetic syndrome . . . chances were that this baby also had "the syndrome." I was alone at the time. I didn't cry much at the doctor's office, but all the way home, a two-hour drive, I was in tears, asking aloud, "Why?"

Barbara

I looked at her tiny face and I knew something was wrong. Her ears were low, her eyes were slanted and puffed, her little face too round. The recognition was instant and that fear at that moment has never left me. The nurse held the baby up and said, "Say hello to Mommy and say goodbye." I asked to be wheeled down to watch them work on my baby and I asked everyone, doctors, nurses, "Is my baby mongoloid?" but no one answered or looked at me. I went back to my room defeated, and after four hours of trying to sleep with the help of pills that didn't work, the doctor came in to tell me he thought my baby had Down syndrome.

Eileen

Although the first time I saw Nicole, I knew in my heart that she didn't look "normal," I tried to deny it. When the doctor confirmed at Nicole's ten-day checkup that she suspected something was "wrong," I was very scared and very depressed.

Sue

Dave and I were together in the delivery room. We knew something was wrong within minutes. I noticed my baby didn't make a sound and had short, stubby fingers and Dave noticed that he "flopped" out rather than coming out tight-fisted like our daughter did. They took the baby into the adjoining room to "look him over." I kept calling out, "What's the matter, where's my baby?" until the neonatologist looked out of the adjoining room and said, "I'll be right out to talk with you in the recovery room." They took me into the recovery room with all the other moms who had just delivered healthy babies, drew a curtain around us and asked, "Does your baby look any different than your little girl did?" My response was "Oh, God no, don't say it. I know what you're going to say." He then merely stated that he was about 97 percent certain that our baby had Down syndrome. We asked to be given some privacy, so they wheeled us into an empty labor room. I felt shocked, pain throughout my whole body, total grief.

Randy

I slumped against the wall and all of a sudden I felt very far away. Sounds became muffled and I felt very scared and alone. . . . Before I went in [to see Jan] I looked at Emily in the incubator with the tubes attached to her and felt as if my heart would just explode from pain. Then I got tough, wiped my tears, and tried to be strong for Jan.

Jeff

The mood in the delivery room was tense and quiet. After suctioning, she cried a weak, high-pitched cry. They worked on her for what seemed a long time and I *was babbling excitedly, "Is she OK? Can I hold her?" . . . The doctor first told me she was a little cold, then he yelled at me to be quiet and let the nurses do their work. . . . They left her in the incubator to warm her and sent Jeff home. . . .*

They brought her to me the next morning and I treasure the hour I spent with her in blissful ignorance. This baby whose picture I had seen [by ultrasound], who I had named and rocked and sang to and talked to for all those months, was finally in my arms. She looked perfect and healthy to me.

An hour later, I woke up in a panic. I had a feeling of overwhelming dread and anxiety. I thought, "What have I done? I can't take care of a baby! I can't be a mother! Who am I kidding?" I called my husband and he came in. The hospital psychiatrist came and prescribed tranquilizers. . . . When Jeff returned with the pediatrician who told me they thought the baby had Down syndrome I felt as if I'd been hit by a truck, like an actual physical blow. I must have been in a completely numb state of shock, because I can't clearly remember my thoughts or feelings at that time. . . . I think I just rocked and cried and stared into space.

Jan

I had amniocentesis in the fourth month of my pregnancy. I received the news that my baby was a girl and that she had Down syndrome from one of the doctors in the clinic. Frank was with me since he knew we'd have the test results that day. My first reaction was disbelief, numbness. I think I just wanted to block it out and carry on as if nothing out of the ordinary was going on.

Frank doesn't really agree with abortion, but after the doctors quoted everything that could be wrong with our baby he didn't want his child to suffer and felt we should abort. I was very torn; I didn't feel abortion was the answer and yet I didn't feel I could raise a child with special needs. I'd seen my baby on the screen for the ultrasound and she was already moving around and kicking. I felt I didn't have the power to make that decision, that it was up to God. In my heart I knew I couldn't terminate this pregnancy, but I checked into what was involved.

Cathie

PREMATURITY AND MEDICAL CONDITIONS

We, as parents, did have a rough time with the ramifications of our son's delivery because we knew it was medical technology that brought him into the world. However, we were convinced after his fight to survive that he was a fighter and God meant for him to live.

Mary and Rick

Significant conditions associated with a disability may sometimes result in premature birth. As a result there may be a combination of medical problems associated with the disabling condition and/or the prematurity. The doctors usually focus their attention on the medical problems first. The disability may or may not be acknowledged and often the fact that the baby is a few days or weeks early is totally ignored. Trudy's experience with her son's doctors from intensive care substantiates the order of "importance" the issues of medical problems, disabilities, and prematurity play in the care of the child. "The doctors zeroed in on Matthew's heart problems, which they considered life-threatening. They overlooked his Down syndrome. I don't know if they overlooked it because they didn't know how to handle it or if they really just devoted themselves 100 percent to the heart because that was their specialty." Parents who give birth prematurely experience that shock which in itself is a childbearing loss. Then they also have to contend with the fact that not only did this baby come too soon, it's not the "fine and perfect" baby they expected.

Parents who have a baby with medical problems will have more complicated feelings to deal with. Babies who have medical complications usually are attached to tubes which prevent parents from holding them. This physical distance from the baby makes it even more difficult to deal with the emotional distancing that parents may be feeling. While doctors hover over the tiny infant desperately trying to save its life, they may ask why these apparently painful techniques are necessary. Doctors are ethically and legally obligated to perform lifesaving techniques on *all* babies; the disability cannot be a reason for diminished intensity of care. Parents who have hoped or prayed that the baby would die may be overwhelmed with guilt as they watch the attempts to save their baby's life.

Some parents may feel that the doctors are treating their baby like a laboratory experiment when they overhear what sound like caustic remarks about the care their infant is receiving. Lexie described the medical professionals in the intensive care unit: "The doctors were very soft-spoken, *very* medical. They didn't offer anything other than what was asked of them." Pam felt:

The doctors were playing a guessing game. They kept telling us Nina was 1 in 100,000 and the only one to have the 4p minus and hydrocephalus. We felt that they were using Nina and documenting everything. In a way this was all right for medical reasons but I think they should be a little more considerate of the parents' feelings. The doctors could have helped more by taking the time to talk *to* us, to let us know exactly what was happening and not to be so *judgmental.*"

If a child or baby has severe medical conditions the treatment often must take place at a major hospital a significant distance from the family home. For Kevin and Ann, the 200-mile round trip to and from the hospital was exhausting, both emotionally and physically; Ann was recovering from a Caesarean delivery. She and Kevin tried to be with Michael when they could; however, Ann felt that the hospital staff was less than supportive: "Even though he was still legally our son, they treated us like we didn't matter or even care about him. I felt alone and afraid."

GRIEVING

> My pediatrician had the saddest look on his face when he told me he highly suspected my baby had Down syndrome. I must have looked like a lunatic as I felt my spirit leave my body for a moment and watched myself respond—laughing.
>
> Eileen

The emotions that wash over parents during the first few days after giving birth to a baby with a disability, or upon receiving the news that their child is disabled, are often overwhelming. For most parents the memories of the early days of pain and grief are almost like a video being played at fast-forward with still shots in between. They vividly remember certain things that happened, yet other events are simply a blur. Most parents cry and cry while trying to remember all the information that is hurled at them from the trail of professionals who appear in and out of their lives.

Most parents go through a grieving process similar to the kind people experience in response to a death, yet it is more complex. Parents need to grieve the "death" of the "expected" baby while, at the same time, trying to learn to accept the "imperfect" baby to which they have given birth. The stages of grief may intermix as they feel pain, anger (why us?), denial ("there must be a mistake, the doctors must be wrong"), and depression. There is no particular "order" to the grieving process and there is no "right" way to grieve.

Many parents will look for a "way out" during this initial grief. They may have suicidal thoughts, thoughts of killing the baby, thoughts of switching name bracelets, or thoughts of leaving the baby somewhere. These are all common reactions. A conversation that took place between one mother and father clearly demonstrates the intensity of these feelings of desperation:

"I'll kill the baby."
"How're you gonna do that?"
"I'll throw it down the stairs."
"That won't kill her, that'll only break her neck."
"Then I'll do it again."

Another mom, Julie, remembers "thoughts of killing both ourselves and our child—to end the pain of life for Hollie and to end the pain of making the decision to have her live with someone else."

Buried beneath all of these emotions is the awareness that decisions must be made. This isn't the time to make permanent decisions, but the consideration of options may help parents feel more control over a situation in which they feel powerless. Looking at options may be an alternate form of seeking a way out. Any options chosen will not take away the pain or immediately return life to normal, but most parents who have examined all of the options available to them seem to build a new life with more resolve.

Parents Talk

The eleven hours between Adam's birth and the time Mary Ann learned of his genetic problem were the longest hours of my life. I remember standing outside the nursery, looking in, and wondering why this had happened to him, to Mary Ann, to me, to our family. One of the nurses asked if I'd like to hold him. I'm sure she felt this would help the bonding process for me. I accepted and sat in a rocker in the nursery, holding Adam for more than an hour. But instead of bonding with him, I argued with myself over whether or not I should suffocate him then and there, thus ending all of our problems. I can't say exactly why I didn't, but I recall giving him back to the nurse, still wondering why I had allowed him to live.

Hank

I wished the baby would die. When I found out he had a heart defect I prayed surgery wouldn't help. I fleetingly thought of suicide, but remembered our older child who needed me.

Mary Ann

In the early months of pregnancy before "the news," I had hoped that if this baby were deformed, it would be miscarried naturally. After I found out that the baby had "the syndrome," I still hoped that something natural would happen to terminate the pregnancy. But nothing happened. I don't remember feeling so depressed that I contemplated taking either my life or the baby's life.

Barbara

I wanted to die for a period of time and then I thought about our son and that if he just went to sleep and never woke up that I could just say that it was God's will and it would have been so much easier on me. I wouldn't have to be strong.

Mary

When the overwhelmingness of the situation became apparent I felt it was a "no-win" situation. I felt that if Hollie's life was to be so hard and so "missing" that it wasn't perhaps worth it for her to live. I wanted at one time for us to be together because I loved her so much that the only way we could be [together] was in death. We could still stay together that way as mother and child in peace.

Julie

We prayed for death. Rebecca died and we cried but were relieved. As we saw no option other than raising her we asked God to take Rachel due to her heart condition.

Beth and Daniel

I woke up every morning sick to my stomach listening for a noise from the bassinet in the next room. Part of me hoped there would be none, that the baby would be dead, and part of me feared he was and that I'd then feel so guilty for wishing it so.

Joanne

I laugh, now, because I never would have gotten away with it [killing the baby], but I had it all figured out. I know I never could have had the heart to go through with it, and, thank God, I came to my senses and realized that this was not the solution to our problem.

Eileen

I wished she would die. I wanted to kill the baby. I don't think I would have done it but I was very, very depressed.

Rona

After seeing Nina suffer so many times I did wish God would take her and she would then be at peace. After Nina was placed in her family care home I went into a deep depression. I contemplated suicide often. Half the time I did not know where I was or what I was doing.

Pam

We wished the baby had never been born. Why didn't I miscarry? We also wished the baby had died after birth so we could have buried him and there would have been no decision to make.

Lauren and Mike

After hearing what Michael would have to go through I really was hoping he would die. I felt that if he was to die at least he wouldn't suffer anymore.

Kevin

I never for a moment wished my baby harm or thought of harming myself. I just wished she had been normal. I fantasized that she was normal.

Jan

I prayed and prayed—I begged God to take my baby, not to make me make the decision. I told Him that He knew I couldn't raise a child like this and that He knew I couldn't abort my baby either. I've never before prayed harder for anything until I begged Him to take my baby and not put me through it.

Cathie

For those first several days and weeks I wished someone would steal our baby. I wished him dead and I wished myself dead.

Randy

I just wanted to wake up from the nightmare. I wished that I could move away, that the baby would die. It would have been a lot easier.

Kathleen

We thought the baby would have been better off dying so we didn't have to face bringing this baby home or giving her up for adoption. She had a major heart defect and was having such a difficult time breathing and eating. It killed us to see her like this. It took us about two or three weeks before we could face up to the fact that she had Down syndrome. Prior to that we told all our other friends and relatives that the baby was in the hospital with a major heart defect. Sometimes, I wonder if we were ashamed or embarrassed, besides being sick.

Lorraine and Warren

Note to New Parents ────────────────────────────────────

You are *not* alone. Whatever you're feeling has been felt by someone else. Any thoughts you might be having are not "bad" thoughts, nor are you a "bad person" for having those thoughts. It's "normal" to feel cheated—your life has been suddenly and drastically changed.

If you've wished your baby dead, don't feel guilty. It's a common reaction to the pain of grief and loss, disappointment and fear. However, if you have suicidal or homicidal thoughts that persist, please get help! If you haven't been connected with a counselor, seek out someone you feel you can trust and who is qualified to work with you to sort through the feelings of grief and loss.

You *do* have options. You can *choose* to care for your child yourself or you can *choose* alternative care. If you're pregnant, you may *choose* abortion, or you may *choose* to continue the pregnancy and then *choose* whether you or someone else will raise your baby.

Your life has changed, but you will make decisions that are right for you and your family and you will build a new life around the decisions you make.

I feel empty
I feel frozen
I feel small, smaller and smaller
I feel buried alive, put to sleep
I feel dead
I feel numb
I feel nothing.

I feel myself under water, unable to move or breathe or
   see light
I feel myself in a place with no top or bottom, a place
   with no walls and no protection
I feel myself trapped in a burning room
I feel myself shredded
I feel myself on fire.

Alla Bozarth-Campbell, Ph.D.
from *Life is Goodbye/Life is Hello*

2

Decisions, Decisions

OPTIONS

> When we asked the director of social services about adoption, she shook her head and stated, "Special needs children just aren't very adoptable." Institutionalization wasn't offered or considered. We didn't wish that as an option—but I know I wished for *something.*
>
> Randy

Exploring options is a healthy way for parents to deal with a situation where they feel backed into a corner. Considering alternatives gives them a feeling that they have at least a small element of control over a situation where they feel helpless.

Years ago, some babies with severe medical complications of disabling conditions such as Down syndrome and spina bifida would not have survived simply because such babies were not treated. Parents of babies who did survive were advised to place them in an institution. Some parents ignored the advice of their physicians and took their babies home. These parents have paved the way for new research which has led to the discovery that children with disabilities reach their potential better in a home environment. Institutions generally no longer accept babies with disabilities, which leads many physicians to imply that the only choice available to parents is to take the baby home. If the diagnosis has been made prenatally, professionals often subtly encourage abortion. Both Cathie and Barbara received a diagnosis through prenatal testing. Neither were given options other than abortion or parenting their children. Both of them thought of adoption as an option and investigated it themselves.

Parents who are searching for options may find it very difficult to get accurate information. Many of the families interviewed felt frustrated and angry at what appeared to be ignorance on the part of many medical professionals. Parents were told: "There are no options." "Foster care is the only other option but not one you'd want to consider." "No one wants to adopt children with special needs." Or, even worse, "How could you think of such a thing?" Parents who are looking for options have to face the scrutiny of some professionals who paternalistically imply that the only acceptable option is to take the baby home. Parents may question: "What's wrong with us? Why can't we just accept this like other parents do?" Feelings of guilt are compounded for parents who may not feel capable of raising their child, but who are advised that it is "the norm."

Most parents do accept their child and his or her condition and continue with their lives. They adjust to the child's disability and love him or her as much, if not more than a "normal" child. These parents find support from other parents and from local agencies and probably will never consider alternative care for their child.

Parents who explore options usually are surprised to learn that there are parents who specifically request to adopt children with disabilities. In fact, many professionals are not aware that there are waiting lists. Rona and Max contacted Little People of America to get information about raising their daughter. They learned that this organization has an adoption coordinator who maintains a list of parents waiting to adopt children born with conditions that result in short stature. Many parents quoted in this book spoke with Janet Marchese of the National Down Syndrome Adoption Exchange, who has a list of thirty to forty prospective adoptive parents. There *are* parents waiting to adopt children with various disabilities, but it may take persistence and networking to connect with the appropriate organization to find them.

When parents hear of a waiting list they sometimes question "What's wrong with us, then, for not wanting our own child?" They may, however, feel some comfort in learning that there are parents out there who are anxious to raise their child for them if they choose adoption.

For other people, learning of a waiting list may help them finalize the decision to parent their child. Parents may reason, "If there are people out there waiting anxiously for a child with this disability, then we can raise our child ourselves."

Couples who feel the need to further explore options shouldn't feel guilty nor should others impose guilt on them. Some parents need more; some need to explore all available options before making a decision for their child and their family. Those who choose to parent their child after looking at options often feel a sense of resolve and acceptance. Parents who choose adoption after carefully considering options usually find peace in knowing that they made an informed choice.

Parents Talk

We had to search for information about adoption; no one at the hospital mentioned it to us. Finally, the social worker at the hospital arranged for a mother of a 5-year-old with Down syndrome to come and speak to us openly and objectively about the decision we were considering. She was very helpful and nonjudgmental and provided us with the phone number for the National Down Syndrome Adoption Exchange. Thank God!!!

Lorraine and Warren

We were deluged by people. The baby was in a high-tech medical center and we talked with a social worker, a geneticist, a pediatric neurologist, a neonatologist. We talked about foster care if we didn't want to take the baby home. Adoption was mentioned but they passed it over.

Rona

From the Little People of America we learned of young little people couples' desire to adopt babies with achondroplasia rather than take a 50 percent risk of an unwanted outcome ("normal" baby—25%, nonviable baby—25%).

Max

It was assumed by all of the professionals that we would bring our son home. No options were given. My doctor just mentioned that if it were twenty years ago, he would be institutionalized automatically. Even though I hadn't received information about adoption, it was always in the back of my mind.

Trudy

I had contacted a lady with the Down Syndrome Association and in talking with her she mentioned Janet Marchese who runs the Down Syndrome Adoption Exchange. I had previously been told that Down syndrome children were not adoptable. This was a glimmer of hope for me because I felt so lost at this point knowing I couldn't abort, but at the same time feeling that I could not handle a child with the special needs with my own problems with depression and struggling to raise my three older children on my own.

Cathie

The agency we adopted Hollie from came over once and literally dropped us like a lead balloon when we needed them for guidance. They said "If this was your birthchild you wouldn't even think of relinquishment."

Julie

A genetic counselor mentioned adoption immediately after we heard the news, but we quickly and adamantly refused to hear about it. We now wish they had been more encouraging of adoption, but there was no material to read about adoption so they gave us a book on how to raise your baby with Down syndrome, a message in itself.

Beth and Daniel

About one-and-a-half years ago, I saw the Jane Wallace Show. . . . This was the first time I knew that there were people who actually wanted to adopt physically and mentally handicapped children. I also learned that there were many children with handicaps in Nicole's preschool that had been adopted. I had these two things in mind when I made the decision for myself to give Nicole up. I had been thinking about it for the last six months or so, and actually made the first phone call two months ago.

Sue

Through my tears I vaguely heard something about options. I couldn't focus on what anyone was saying. My mother, husband, and I made an appointment to see a social worker the next day and I sat there listening to her. For some reason, I don't know why, she was annoying the hell out of me, I guess because I thought she "had it all." My husband did the talking and I remember thinking, "Who would want to adopt a baby with Down syndrome?"

Eileen

We got information about adoption through a couple who had adopted two children with Down syndrome as well as two other children with learning disorders. We had asked the obstetrician if adoption was available and he only answered by shaking his head "no," as if to say, "Who would want him?"

Hank and Mary Ann

One of my husband's work associates had a retarded son who lived at home for his early years and had to be institutionalized in his later life. His associate said to me: "You may hate me for what I have to say, but don't bring the baby home." I had never heard anyone ever say that or even thought people actually did that. But he planted that thought and we took it from there.

Lexie

Although the social workers were very supportive of our consideration of adoption, most of the medical professionals treated us with pity—"What kind of people would want him, if you don't?" We kept asking if anyone else had ever gone through with an adoption, and they would shake their heads and say, "I'm sorry, you're my only experience with something like this."

Joanne and Bob

We could either have the operation to close up Michael's spine or bring him home with an 80 percent chance of death and give him drugs to keep him comfortable until he was dead. Adoption was brought up the next day. The timing could have been better. If we had known adoption was a possibility we might have elected to have surgery done earlier rather than struggle with our emotions trying to decide if death would be better for all of us.

Ann

My obstetrician gave me a big pep talk about the wonderful things Down syndrome kids can achieve these days with early intervention and walked out. The doctor from the genetic center gave me a book and a pep talk. Neither even ac-knowledged that there was any option other than raising Emily. I found out about the availability of adoptive families by chance.

Jan

The medical staff set up a meeting for us involving all of Nina's caretakers. At this meeting we were informed on the pros and cons of Nina's condition. They made it clear to us that she needed extensive care and that she could be placed in a hospital. More information concluded that these hospitals did not care for in-fants. Someone in that meeting mentioned a family care program with a develop-mental center. My husband and I left this meeting not knowing what to do.

Pam

There were two options given. One, I could take this baby home—which is what the hospital professionals really pushed for, or, two, give the baby over to the State Department of Social Services and they would find a foster home for the baby. I would have no contact with the baby or even know anything about the foster family. Another option had been mentioned—the Jewish Parents and Chil-dren's Services—which sounded like a good option to us because we are Jewish and I thought a family through this agency would be screened well. There was no one available through this agency so we were back to the first two options.

Lauren

After I dismissed abortion as a viable option, I started to think of other alterna-tives. I had read, and seen on television, reports of families who had welcomed handicapped children into their families. . . . I checked out books on adoption, all written with prospective adoptive parents in mind. . . . Nowhere did I see any information on how to go about releasing one's own handicapped child for adop-tion. I thought that perhaps I was crazy to even think such a thing.

Barbara

EARLY DECISIONS

I was looking at Emily in the nursery and standing next to my father-in-law. We were both very teary and I said to him I didn't think Jan could take raising a Down syndrome baby. Then I stopped and said I didn't think I could do it emotionally either.

Jeff

No permanent decisions should be made while in an extreme state of distress, but parents probably will be faced with several smaller deci-sions that need to be made immediately. Some decisions about care for a healthy baby will need to be made soon after birth: "Will you breast-feed? Will you take your baby home with you or seek alternative care?" Decisions like these may not be necessary for parents of babies who have health problems—breast-feeding may not be possible and most likely the baby will be in the intensive care nursery for several days or even months. A diagnosis made prenatally requires parents to make other kinds of decisions. Parents of children who have a diagnosis after several months or years face even different decisions.

Most of the decisions that need to be made will not be right or wrong, black or white, but *no* decision should be made without obtaining accurate information. Parents will need to gather information from as many sources as possible. Decisions should be made without pressure from outsiders. Most parents have a sense of what "feels" right, even when in the throes of grief. Eileen says, "We couldn't do what another couple did if we felt it was not right for us. We had to dig deep into each other's hearts and souls and pull the answers out."

Getting to Know the Baby

> When people looked at my son and said, "What a beautiful baby!," I'd want to scream at them, "Can't you see it?" But a few weeks later I, too, saw the beauty, the precious, lopsided smile and the charming personality.
>
> Joanne

Parents who are considering adoption may think that it would be easier to never see or hold their infant. Although this may be true for some people, the majority of parents who choose an adoption plan for their child usually recover more quickly and feel more at peace if they have spent even a small amount of time with their newborn.

Many parents do find that when they get to know their child they learn to love the baby so much that the pain of living with a child with a disability eases. Mary advises, "I don't think you can truly appreciate the baby even in a few months. Though we experienced peace at our decision to keep Lanier we had to deal with a lot of pain and hurt for our child." Others find it extremely painful to watch as their baby struggles for life. Trudy's son was extremely sick, and as she watched over him for the first four months she remembers, "I went through the process of everyday living like a zombie. My spirit was broken. One day I just broke down and cried to my girlfriend that I could not go on anymore." Still others feel a need to find love for their infant before they can let go. Joanne believed, "I needed time to get over the shock, to educate myself, and to give Brian a chance to be part of our family or I wouldn't be able to live with myself in the future." And others, like Jan and Jeff, make a firm, early decision and find it too painful to have continued contact with the baby. Jan says, "I knew I was giving Emily up and that holding her and feeding her would make giving her up even more agonizing. . . .

I asked our friends and one of my brothers to rock, feed, cuddle, sing to, massage, and kiss Emily every day."

Whatever decision parents make they may want pictures at some time in the future. One mother decided several weeks after her baby was adopted that she wanted pictures and had difficulty obtaining them. It caused her a great deal of anguish that might have been avoided. Although Jan didn't continue to have contact with her baby after choosing an adoption plan, she reveals, "We took photos which I will treasure forever." Parents who feel they can't take their own pictures may want to consider having someone else take them and save them in case they change their minds later.

Breast-feeding

> I chose to breast-feed because it just seemed right; I'd had such a positive experience with Casey. I knew it would give Jake added benefits in building up immunities and with his potential physical problems he'd need all the help we could give him.
>
> Randy

Feeding difficulties are common among newborns with complex medical and developmental problems. These infants may have altered oral-motor structure, low muscle tone, and/or poor coordination. These issues together with other medical problems may interfere with plans to breast-feed. It can be very frustrating for a mother who is experiencing all of the emotions about her baby's disability and who is probably not getting enough rest or nutrients herself to try to breast-feed a baby who appears uninterested or is having difficulty because of his or her condition.

Many mothers who have babies healthy enough to make the attempt at breast-feeding persist in trying, anyway. Some mothers have a concern about providing natural immunity. Others feel that breast-feeding might increase the bond that they hope will happen. One mother says, "I wanted to try to feel some of that attachment I had felt for my daughter." Another didn't breast-feed because, "I wanted to distance myself in case I did decide to give him up or lost him to his heart defects." Some mothers choose not to breast-feed because, as Lauren says, "I had no intention to breast-feed. I didn't with my first or third. I like to bottle-feed."

Pumping breast milk and then bottle-feeding is an alternative for those babies who do not succeed at breast-feeding or who must be tube-fed. Lorraine and Beth pumped milk for about two or three weeks for their babies who were fed through tubes. Lorraine stopped because "it became too emotional considering how upset I already was." By the time

Beth's baby was able to nurse, she was used to gavage (tube-feeding) and bottles and wouldn't breast-feed. There is no right or wrong choice, but there is a choice that is best for both the mother and her baby.

GATHERING INFORMATION

> There are so few decisions in life that are permanent . . . but this decision is so final. I wanted to be sure and to know that whatever decision I made that I could live with myself for the rest of my life.
>
> Lauren

Many people who receive the news that their child has a disability may have preconceived notions of what that means. These ideas may have been based on childhood experiences, outdated information from magazines or books, or possibly on conversations with people who knew someone with the disability. Most are simply unknowledgeable of the facts. Joanne says, "My only knowledge of Down syndrome was a childhood memory of a neighbor, a girl who couldn't speak and made grunting noises. She was seldom taken from the house and when she was out in public she would grab at anyone nearby and give them a choking hug."

Ideally, information gathering begins with the delivery of "the news." Informed doctors, nurses, and social workers should provide updated information about the baby's condition immediately. Professionals also should have information available for parents who are considering alternative care. It is very important that parents gather information to help them make an informed choice.

The following suggestions are offered to help parents learn all they can about their baby's condition:

1. *Read current literature.* Much of the literature about disabilities that is readily available is outdated. Some parents are fortunate enough to have current literature provided to them by physicians or by other parents. Others may have to do the searching themselves. The nearest genetics center should be able to provide the most up-to-date literature. Doctors, social workers, and parent support groups can help locate current materials. Be suspicious of material that is over ten years old. It may provide inaccurate information.

Current resources often are not found on the shelves of the local library or in stock in a bookstore. A reliable bookstore will order books; find one that will assure timely receipt. The books and articles listed in the appendix of this book are those suggested by parents who have "been there," though none address the issues surrounding the adoption choice.

Magazine articles are often more current. Several articles have been written by parents who have children with disabilities. The *Reader's Guide to Periodical Literature* in a local library lists magazine articles (look under the title "disability" or the specific name of the child's disability). A reference librarian also can be helpful. The latest magazines often are stored in the library.

2. *Meet with families of children with disabilities.* If a child has a rare disability, it may be difficult to meet with families who have children with a similar condition. It may take persistence, several telephone calls, and/or connection to a national organization or clearinghouse. It would be likelier to find someone who has experienced a *similar* situation. The people recommended previously could help locate organizations, as will the resources listed in the appendix.

More common conditions such as Down syndrome offer an opportunity to share with other parents and sometimes to observe children. Many communities now have a parent-to-parent support network, sometimes organized through the Association for Retarded Citizens or another advocacy organization. The local genetics center, a doctor, or a hospital social worker should have information on how to get in touch with parents who are raising a child with a similar condition. These parents can be a valuable resource. Not only do they provide current information, but they also can introduce you to their children to help you modify any preconceived notions.

Parent support groups often have gatherings at least once or twice a year, and some as often as once a month. Many parents have been fortunate enough to be invited to attend one of these get-togethers. Most support groups have these meetings either as a formal program with workshops and speakers or as an informal gathering such as a family-oriented picnic.

3. *Observe children with disabilities.* In some larger communities there are schools for children with disabilities where it is possible to observe children of varied ages. It also may be possible to talk with teachers who work with these children on a daily basis. In most communities children with disabilities are mainstreamed, or integrated, into regular preschools and schools as much as possible so that it might be more difficult to observe large numbers of children at one time. Regular schools may allow visits and observations after obtaining permission from the children's parents. To arrange for a visit, call the local school district and ask for the director of special education.

4. *Talk with parents who considered an adoption plan.* Most parents who considered adoption felt a need to talk to others who had similar feelings. There are so many questions to be answered, so many emotions surrounding this issue. Unfortunately, it is difficult to find other people in one locality who have even considered adoption as an option, and even rarer to find someone to talk to who has chosen the adoption route.

Organizations such as the National Down Syndrome Adoption Exchange provide invaluable networking services. An organization such as this should be able to give names and telephone numbers of parents who lived through a decision-making process. Most parents find it helpful to talk to parents from both "sides"—those who made the decision to raise their child and those who chose adoption. Many parents found these contacts to be a lifesaver. The connections often were several hundred miles away, but the large telephone bills incurred were very worthwhile.

5. *Talk with parents who have adopted.* A frequent question new parents ask is, "Who would want to adopt our baby?" Many new parents found it helpful to talk with parents who adopted a child, or children, with a disability. Most adoptive parents are open, giving people who freely talk about their reasons for choosing to adopt a child with special needs. It is often possible to find parents in a nearby area who have adopted a child or children with disabilities. Special needs adoption agencies, such as those listed in the appendix, should be able to provide names of families who have adopted and who would be willing to talk with parents considering this option. Chapter 6 introduces four adoptive families and describes some of their reasons for choosing to adopt a child with a disability.

6. *Talk with professionals.* Professionals who work with children with disabilities can be a valuable source of information. Randy and Dave found a school psychologist to be an important source of information and very supportive. Another family found the early infant stimulation teacher to be particularly supportive; she also put the parents in touch with other families. Special education directors at local schools can also be helpful.

For many parents, meeting with other parents and getting to know children with a similar disability gives them enough information to make a decision. Many parents accept the circumstances and although most do go through a period of sadness and grief, grieving the loss of the child they expected, they grow to love the child to whom they have given birth. They soon become wound up in the day-to-day care required for any infant, or child, incorporating the special care as part of the daily routine.

SHOULD PARENTS TAKE THE BABY HOME FROM THE HOSPITAL?

We were told that if we didn't take our baby home, we would have to surrender him to the state with no further contact. We wouldn't even know anything about the foster family. The publicity about foster homes in our locality was bad—abuse, neglect—so we took him

home. We couldn't just leave him to the wolves; he was still our flesh
and blood.

Lauren and Michael

Parents who are considering the option of adoption often ask if they
should take the baby home from the hospital. If the baby has medical
problems, the parents are afforded additional time to educate themselves before the baby is released. Lorraine and Warren's baby was in
intensive care for three months. They share, "We were thankful that we
didn't have to bring her home; it was a blessing in disguise. We had
plenty of time to make our decision and we wanted to see our precious
little girl go straight to a good, loving, permanent home." Even if the
baby is healthy, some hospitals will allow the baby to remain there an
extra day or two to give the parents time to think and to do some of the
necessary research. Randy and Dave left Jake in the hospital for four
days before deciding to take him home.

One concern many parents have is that if they take the baby home they
will become too attached to go through with an adoption. Others have
chosen to take their baby home, to take time to get to know their child, to
give themselves time to work through some of the grief. Parents who
choose adoption may feel more at peace if they have had their child at
home even for a short period of time, but each individual couple must
make the decision that's right for them.

Siblings of the baby also have been awaiting the birth of a new brother
or sister. Many parents reason that if their baby never comes home, their
other children will not get attached. Even very young children have
some awareness about the pregnancy. If the mother goes into the hospital to have a baby and the children never see it, the mystery may cause
them to conjure up all kinds of possibilities. If children are old enough to
ask questions, parents still will need to come up with explanations for
"What happened to the baby?" Taking the baby home can add to a sibling's confusion if an adoption plan is decided upon, but there are many
other factors to consider.

IF NOT HOME, WHERE DOES THE BABY GO?

Foster care is good because sometimes you have to get away from
something in order to make a clear decision.

Mary and Rick

If a baby is ready to leave the hospital before parents have had a chance
to explore options, they may need to find a temporary care home. Nearly
all parents who have considered adoption advise new parents to take
time. It takes much longer than a few days to recover from the emotional

turmoil that the news has most certainly caused. If parents choose not to take their baby home, or if they take the baby home and find they need a break, there are alternate care options available.

Babies with some disabilities were institutionalized in the past; a few doctors may still suggest this form of care. Institutionalization is no longer an option for most infants with disabilities, or one that would be recommended by most specialists. Parents who ask about institutionalization for an infant probably will be advised to consider foster care or told to take the baby home.

Foster Care, Respite Care, Guardianship

Foster care and *respite care* may have slightly different definitions and stipulations depending on the state in which parents reside. Regulations may even differ within a state.

Foster care is usually formal and sponsored by the state or an adoption agency. Parents must sign papers that appoint the state or agency as temporary custodians of the child. Parents still retain certain legal rights to the child. The parents reserve the right to see the child as long as certain stipulations, outlined on the papers they sign, are followed (for example, twenty-four-hour notice). They also may take the child back home to live at any time—again, if they've followed specified guidelines. Parents are asked to authorize permission for medical care. The foster parents usually are screened by the state or agency and are paid a stipend for the care they are providing. Usually, expenses for formula, clothing, and other necessities for the baby are incurred by the agency or state, but, sometimes, agencies may ask the birthparents to absorb some or all of the costs.

Foster care in some localities is excellent. In other areas there may be bad publicity that causes concern for birthparents. Babies within the foster care system could be caught up in varying degrees of red tape and may be moved from home to home. Birthparents also should be cautious of local regulations and the stigmatizing effect foster care may have (for instance, usually foster care is used for cases of abuse, neglect, or delinquency or when parents are admitting their inability to care for the child).

Respite care is less formal and intended to provide families with temporary relief from the care of a child with a disability. In some places respite care is only an emergency care program. In others, it may be a form of specialized babysitting. Respite usually is intended for short time periods, but different localities offer different programs.

Respite services usually are provided through a developmental disabilities program or family support services and are usually state funded. Families who agree to provide respite often have had some experience with children with disabilities. Again, parents retain all legal rights to the child and may see the child according to predetermined guidelines. Information about respite care usually can be obtained from local agencies for people with disabilities.

Guardianship is a more permanent form of care used for longer time periods. The child lives with a family who will physically care for him, but legal responsibility is retained by the parents. Birthparents generally give the guardians a power of attorney but it could be withdrawn at any time.

Like respite and foster care, guardianship may be governed by different agencies. Rules and regulations may be different depending upon where one lives. Names for these arrangements may also vary. For example, Pam and Rich's birthchild lives in a "family care home," a guardianship agreement arranged by their county's developmental center.

Guardianship arrangements may not always be regarded as being in the best interest of the child. There is no "permanency" for the child. Problems could arise if health care providers do not know whom to recognize as the legal caretakers, especially if there is a difference of opinion between the guardians and the birthparents about medical care. Pam admits that a decision she and Rick made about Nina's care was disturbing for the family care mother: "I can understand how she felt at the time. She cared for Nina and loved her very much but could not have any say in making such an important decision in Nina's life."

Families considering alternative care should thoroughly check out the system before signing papers to allow their child to live elsewhere. It might be necessary to seek out a lawyer who is knowledgeable about family matters and about state laws concerning persons with disabilities.

Other Forms of Substitute Care

Some families make arrangements for another family to provide care for their infant while they investigate options and educate themselves. Some accept offers from extended family members to care for their child during this time period. Parents should be cautious of less structured forms of care and not feel pressured by family members to use this option if they don't want to. In a state of vulnerability, parents may be very tempted to take the "easy way out" and accept offers from friends and family. Although this form of substitute care may work well for some families, it may not work for others. These situations could become much more complicated later on and cause more distress for the parents. Parents should be cautious of legalities that might judge them as abandoning their child. Again, a family lawyer might be necessary to write up an agreement.

Parents Talk

We took Brian home and he stayed with us for six weeks. Then we used foster care until the adoption was finalized. Our daughter was almost 3 at the time. I have to admit that it has been difficult explaining to her why he is no longer with us, but I haven't regretted my decision to bring him home.

Joanne

We brought our son home after two months of intensive care. We felt that it would be the ultimate test—to bring him home and then to place him elsewhere. We then placed him in foster care for ten days with the people who would have been the adoptive parents. They allowed us two weeks to make a decision.

Mary and Rick

I brought Matthew home from the hospital because I didn't have any other option presented. He was 4 months old and back in the hospital when I made my decision. He went from the hospital to the adoptive home but was technically in foster care, with his adoptive parents, just until his final papers came through.

Trudy

If we had brought Michael home even for a short period of time we could have damaged him more than he already was. His chances of reaching his full potential could have been hurt beyond repair if everything was not done right, from the start.

Kevin

[Michael has spina bifida. He had surgery to repair the hole in his spine, more to place a shunt in his brain. He required special care when being held and/or fed.]

We went to a mental health counselor twice. We haven't gone back. The woman kept saying, "Isn't there some way you can still keep custody and have him somewhere else?" To me she meant to institutionalize my baby and I flatly refused to do this. My son needed parents who could take care of him and love him.

Ann

The baby needed eye surgery and had to stay in the hospital so it gave us time to figure out what we were going to do. Once we decided on adoption we wanted her to start her life with her new family. If we were not to be her parents, we would find her the best and she would go to them immediately upon release and start her life. After being in the hospital for three weeks, she needed loving arms around her.

Eileen and Louis

The baby came home with us. Leaving her there was never a real option for us. Our initial reaction had been that we were the best parents for her and we thought we could raise her and get close to her. Associates who were very supportive hired a baby nurse for us for three weeks.

We didn't use foster or respite care. Foster care may be a good thing for some people but we didn't want her handled by a lot of people, passed around, or some place temporary.

Rona and Max

Emily needed much specialized care and we realized that having her at home for even a short amount of time would have made it incredibly difficult to give her up.

Jeff

My husband had been a caseworker in children's services in our county for years. . . . We felt we would be treated honestly and respectfully and that our child would get the best placement possible. We were half right. As soon as we signed the papers, social services assumed a parental role over both Emily and us. They told us Emily would be placed with a family that knew she was available for adoption. . . . We found out later that the family thought they were only providing foster care. I was told that the new mother was asked to visit Emily in the hospital and that she refused. I found out later that she was never asked. . . . By lying to us they prevented us from making fully informed decisions about our daughter based on reality. They justified these lies by saying they were protecting the adoptive family in case we changed our minds.

Jan

The baby was in intensive care for approximately four weeks. Once we made adoption an option, we couldn't mentally bring her home.

Lexie

At the time they weren't sure she had Down syndrome. The doctors said to take her home and love her. When I heard about adoption, I knew right away that was what I wanted. I called all over the state to different organizations until I got in touch with the National Down Syndrome Adoption Exchange.

Kathleen

The couple we had talked with who had adopted other children with special needs offered, and we accepted, to care for him until we made our final decision. It was a friendly arrangement, not a formal foster care situation. We felt the baby should be out of our home before signing papers, in order to assess any "second thought" feelings.

Mary Ann and Hank

Nina was placed in the first family care home when she was 3 months old. We decided to use family care because it is different from foster care. You do not give up your rights as parents. Every decision must be decided by the parents. For us, this was the best way to go. We felt we were not giving Nina up totally and we could decide to do whatever was best for her.

Pam

Jake was about 5 weeks old when we decided to place him for adoption, but we felt that we needed a final "test" to see how we'd do with him out of the house. We chose respite over foster care because some foster homes are "the pits" and with respite there was no paperwork. One of the families we had met who had a 7-year-old child with Down syndrome and eleven other children volunteered to care for Jake while we made sure of our decision. It worked well for us; we knew he'd be getting infant stimulation and that we could call or visit at any time.

Randy and Dave

Two weeks before my baby was born I found out she would be coming home with me until I was able to take her to her adoptive parents. Because of the open adoption she had to leave the hospital with me. I was hysterical over this, but felt so strong in my decision [the adoption plan] that I could handle it. I was concerned about my other children and the effect it would have on them, but we were all in counseling so I felt we'd get through it. At the time I felt it would give me the first couple weeks with her that no one could ever take from me and I didn't want her in foster care before going to her new family.

Cathie

Note to New Parents

In addition to the grief you are experiencing you're probably feeling very confused. Try to take control over smaller decisions about your baby's care. The decision of whether to take your baby home is not as difficult to make as a final, permanent decision, but it is one you should consider carefully. You must do what feels right for you and your own family. Don't let anyone pressure you into any decisions that don't feel right to you.

It is very important that you educate yourself about your child's disability and what it will mean to you, your child, and your family. If you continue to consider adoption as an option, the more you learn about your child's condition, the more confident you will be of the decision you make.

Always take time to assess your own situation carefully. You *can* make intelligent, reasoned decisions even when you're in a state of grief.

Loving the Body

I have lost my place.
My body has become
a foreign country.
I no longer know
its maps or rules.

What languages it speaks
are silent to me or
frighten me to silence
by their strangeness.

They seem harsh.
They come from nerve,
and grate.

Even muscle groans
under their sounds.
Skin erupts in the effort
of trying to understand.

I am dried out
from loss of tears,
And sometimes
there are screams.

I grow suddenly dizzy,
caught in the white-out
of an inner tundra storm.
Without focus I cannot tell
if I am going somewhere
or holding still.

I want to move freely
in this country and
live here again.
I want to respond well
to its voices and weathers,
learn its new laws.
I want to feel its welcome again.
I want to be unafraid and peaceful
and know that, after all,
I was born here.

I need an interpreter in my own skin.
Friend, help me to find and keep place here.
Be doctor or lover.
Hold me, and remind me how.

Alla Bozarth-Campbell, Ph.D.
from *Life is Goodbye/Life is Hello*

3

Building a Support Network

SUPPORT SYSTEMS

> If someone told me they "knew what I was going through" I
> would get mad and not open up, but if they said they didn't fully
> understand but were trying to feel our pain, I felt I could trust and
> talk with them.
>
> Eileen

Parents who are considering adoption are making what is probably the
biggest decision of their lives. They may feel an intense aloneness and
will need all of the support they can get. They probably will need assistance in gathering information or finding services. They may need help
with the logistics of day-to-day life—simple things like making meals can
be a strain when someone is in a state of grief. They also may need someone to help them care for their other children while they try to educate
themselves or while they visit their baby in the hospital or in a temporary care home. They probably will need a third person to listen, to help
them sort out their confusion, and to provide emotional comfort. For
some families the people who will provide support are obvious; others
have to search for the type of support they most need.

Families find support from various sources and often different sources
provide for different needs. For some, extended families offer the most
assistance. Others find doctors to be particularly helpful. Many depend
on other parents, usually new friends from parent support groups or
networks. Families must look for the support that meets their most immediate needs.

A great deal of support often can be found from extended family and
from partners. Indeed, many individuals responded that their best sup-

port came from their spouse. However, this chapter will focus on non-family support systems. The support available from family members, as well as more complex issues that are created with family interactions, are addressed in more detail in Chapter 5.

COUNSELING

> It was pointed out to me in therapy that Michael felt just as bad as I about Adam, but he expressed it differently. I was very open with my emotions and Michael kept a lot to himself. Our psychologist taught me each person deals with things differently.
>
> Lauren

Parents who have given birth to a child with a disability usually experience stages of grief similar to those associated with a death—the child they dreamed of "died." Most parents need to mourn the death of their dream child before they can totally accept the child to whom they have given birth. During these stages of grief parents describe an emotional roller coaster—a whole range of feelings that may seem overwhelming. If parents become familiar with "normal" stages of grieving, then they will be less likely to feel as if they are "going crazy." A counselor who is experienced in these issues can help couples sort out these normal reactions from those which may need to be examined more carefully. Books on grief and loss such as those listed in the appendix also may be helpful.

Ideally, parents should be connected with a counselor soon after being delivered the news that their baby or child has a disability. Mothers who receive the news prenatally should have received genetic counseling before the procedure. The same counselor usually will provide follow-up support. Parents who have a newborn should be provided with a hospital social worker or a person who assumes a similar role. Hospital chaplains also may be helpful. Professionals who are unable to provide ongoing support should offer names and numbers of appropriate counseling professionals with whom parents can connect. Even parents who seem accepting may need counseling after they leave the protective hospital environment.

Couples who are considering an adoption plan face a heart-wrenching decision. Most couples find it necessary to seek someone to serve as an unbiased sounding board. Counseling support may be obtained from any combination of the following:

1. *Social workers* who work in an adoption agency, in a hospital, or for obstetric physicians are very experienced with the emotional issues surrounding the loss of a child. Those who work specifically in adoption agencies also should be knowledgeable about legalities.

2. *Clergy people* obviously would be helpful in dealing with spiritual issues.

3. *Doctors* sometimes offer informal counseling. Families often find a great deal of support from their family doctor, pediatrician, or obstetrician.

4. *Psychologists and psychiatrists* may help parents resolve personal issues. Crises often unearth unpleasant memories and family experiences from childhood. Many parents have a need to try to resolve some of these issues before making a decision. Persons who have experience counseling people about grief and loss are usually the most helpful.

The degree the counselor holds is not nearly as important as the empathy, understanding, and experience in dealing with issues of this nature. Counselors who listen, who do not imply that they have all the answers, and who do not exhibit any subtle, or blatant, forms of judgment are most helpful. Many families found it necessary to talk with two or three different people before deciding upon the one who would be right for them.

PARENT SUPPORT GROUPS

> I got in contact with about twenty different families who I took turns calling, in my various stages of desperation, during the three months Rachel was in intensive care nursery. They were helpful, but when I asked the genetic counselor for names of parents who'd chosen adoption, she couldn't give me any.
>
> Beth

Parent support groups are very valuable to parents who are raising their children with disabilities. They have the most accurate information and the real-life experience to relate what day-to-day life with a child with a disability is like. They often can provide parents with names of authorities. Some may even offer help in avoiding any "red tape" involved in enrolling the child in services. In most communities the person in charge will try to match the new family with a similar family. If this match doesn't work, then they will try again. For most parents, the "experienced family" gives them the support they need to make it through the first few weeks and to get their lives back together.

Parents from the support groups are not often supportive of choosing an adoption plan for a child. Some of the parents interviewed found people from these groups who were helpful, who provided information about adoption services, who continued to be supportive in spite of the consideration of another choice; others didn't. The people who are active in these groups are usually very dedicated individuals. They may see parents who are considering adoption as a threat to all that they believe. Some of them may feel a sense of failure if they haven't "talked" new parents "into" keeping the baby when they feel so positive about the experience.

The parents who feel so positive about their experience want to help new parents realize that the grief subsides with time—that life does go on—and to assure the new parents that they have found happiness with their child. Unfortunately, many of the parents interviewed felt they were being "brainwashed," that "they" were telling only the "good" parts of raising a child with a disability. Cathie remembers reading the book *Babies with Down Syndrome* and feeling that the whole book was "so up, so happy—just peaches and roses. I needed to hear more of the down side, more of the heartaches and hardships. I felt the book needed to be more realistic—tell us about the bad times." But, now, Cathie says, "I wish I could tell you more of the heartaches, but I can't. So far every-thing is up and I know when I refer to Angela, it's all up, all the happi-ness and love she brings."

In the initial state of grief some new parents may be extremely sensitive and feel totally inadequate. In a state of vulnerability, feelings referred to as "paranoia" are common. Supportive parents who are enthusiastic about raising a child with a disability may "turn off" new parents. Par-ents who feel totally overwhelmed with feelings of anger, fear, guilt, and depression often find it difficult to relate to these experienced parents who seem so upbeat and positive.

Parents Talk

Some of them [supportive parents] felt that given time we would realize that raising our child . . . would be the only decision we could live with and they were right.

Mary and Rick

I called one mother from the support group and she mentioned me to the others in the group and after that I was constantly on the phone with them. For the most part, they were helpful, informative, and supportive. None of them said they had considered adoption and spoke very little about it with me.

Randy

We were in touch with the Down Syndrome Congress who empathized with us but encouraged us to keep this baby. There were no local parent support groups, but the parents we called who had placed their babies for adoption were very supportive. We wish there were support groups for people like us who surrender their child.

Lauren and Michael

I was unaware of any [support groups] nor did I seek them out. Three years later one of my high school friends, who I had lost touch with, had a Down syndrome child. Knowing her pain I contacted her immediately. She has been my support ever since.

Lexie

We began to think that the supportive parents were doing everything in their power to convince us that we should keep our baby. . . . After our decision was made, one of the women who I had felt close to always seemed to have something more important to do than to speak with me when I called. I felt so isolated—my other friends didn't have any true understanding of what I'd been through. I'd been caught up in this new world of physical therapy and infant stimulation for four months and suddenly had no one to talk to about it. A mother who adopted a child with Down syndrome became, and continues to be, a major source of support.

Joanne

We didn't go after support from the local support groups. I needed constructive advice. I was tired of explaining the whole story to someone who did not have to know. I needed to know about Down syndrome adoption. *They didn't and I didn't want to waste my time.*

Eileen

I belonged to an ARC support group at the time, but I do not remember sharing any information about my dilemma with anyone in the group. I did gain support from knowing other parents of handicapped children, most of whom were worse than my son. Just knowing these people and seeing them face their day-to-day struggles with courage, patience, and, above all, a sense of humor gave me some inner strength and hope.

Barbara

The local parent support was all people raising their children with achondroplasia. One was a psychologist, supportive of our right to choose adoption. Another family seemed very unhappy; they were still crying. We didn't feel that the third family was doing a good job raising their child.

Rona

I spent hours on the phone talking to several parents through our local Down Syndrome Association. They were very supportive. They not only talked about the good times, but also the rough times.

Cathie

There were no support groups that I know of at the time of Nina's birth.

Pam

I got invaluable help from a woman who is the head of the Down syndrome parents' support group in our county. This woman . . . was warm, supportive, informative, honest, *and nonjudgmental. She loves her son, who has Down syndrome, and is glad she has him, yet she respected my right to make my own decision about Emily. She helped me by acting as a liaison to the new family.*

Jan

[A woman who had relinquished her baby] gave us articles and books that would not push us one way or the other with our decision. She was the only one who knew our loss. We had different birth defects with our children but the end result and the pain was still the same.

Ann

MEDICAL COMMUNITY

My OB met with us after we requested it and she was touched. Ours was the first baby with Down syndrome she had ever delivered in her ten-year practice. And of all the hundreds of amnios she has done, there has never been a miscarriage or news of a fetus with DS. Why me? I felt so cheated.

Lorraine

Many parents find a great deal of support from their obstetrician, pediatrician, or family doctor. Most doctors are compassionate and concerned. Many give out home phone numbers and offer informal counseling. Many call new parents on a daily basis to check up on them and on the baby.

Doctors are human and each will have personal opinions and prejudices. Many people have been brought up to regard doctors as gods, expecting that a doctor's advice is carved in stone. In a state of vulnerability if a doctor even subtly expresses an opinion, parents may feel pressured to follow that suggestion. Even if parents feel that the doctor has no right to tell them what to do, it is difficult to question his or her advice. Joanne was very hurt when her pediatrician, whom she respected and trusted, lectured her about the possible repercussions should they consider adoption: "How will you ever explain this to your daughter?" (Explanations for siblings are addressed in Chapter 5.) Barbara felt resentment for doctors who advised her to get an abortion: "They were ironically the ones who knew me the least. I think I would have also resented them if they told me I should keep my baby." Eileen and Louis learned several months after they chose an adoption plan for their baby that their doctor had lived through a similar experience several years ago. They wondered why he hadn't told them. They had interpreted his lack of warmth and discomfort with them as judgment. Instead, he hurt deeply for them, remembering the pain through which he and his wife had gone.

Pam and Richard felt very confused and distraught by the conflicting advice offered by the various doctors involved in Nina's care:

My husband and I did not know where to turn for advice. One doctor told us she would be lucky if she lived to be 1 year old. Another told us she would not make it past 3. After the first shunt was placed, her head-size decreased and fluid was being released. A doctor told us Nina's head would be almost like a normal child and that she would be slightly handicapped. After this conversation, my husband and I had hope. Only after several CT scans and conflicting reports from specialists and doctors did our hope fade away.

They felt that if there had been one doctor to sit down with them and discuss the situation it would have given them the opportunity to think more clearly.

Lauren and Michael found a new pediatrician after their experience. Their first "couldn't even face us. He would look down at the ground when he spoke to us. He never even called to see how our other daughter was dealing with the loss of her baby after we made our decision." Jan's obstetrician cut her off as she started to tell him about their adoption choice for Emily. He angrily said, "If that's what you've decided I don't want to hear about it. Don't try to justify yourself to me!!!" and stormed out of the room. Jan later learned that he couldn't have birth-children and suspected that he thought she should be happy with any baby she got. He, however, had chosen to adopt a "normal" child. Jan felt his judgmental attitude and cruelty were unprofessional and unforgivable and chose another doctor.

It is important for parents to keep themselves surrounded by professionals who are supportive and to avoid, when possible, those who are not. It may be necessary to seek out new health care professionals. Many parents learn from their experience to be more assertive in the medical treatment that they and their families receive. They learn to communicate with physicians on a more equal basis, to accept that medical professionals are human, and to choose physicians to whom they feel they can relate.

Parents Talk

Our pediatrician was very touched by our experience. He was willing to do whatever he could to help and called us at home to see how we were doing.

We felt that many of the nurses at the hospital became cold towards us after they heard what we were considering. This hurt very much! They were all able to go home to their "normal" children, but they were judging us. How could they? Couldn't they see the despair and grief on our faces?

Lorraine and Warren

All of the medical professionals and therapists have been super to us. They were totally unbiased and always seemed very encouraging about our son's po-

*tential and they stressed that his healthy heart would be such a plus in his devel-
opment.*

Mary and Rick

*I have no told any of Nicole's doctors what we are doing. As for what they
could have done better, I wish they had been more straightforward with me about
Nicole's chances of leading a normal life. I got a lot of "we'll have to wait and
see," or "time will tell," or "maybe she'll catch up," when all the time I believe
they knew Nicole was always going to be considerably delayed.*

Sue

*My son's doctors and nurses judged us because we had originally chosen not to
treat our son. I understood their point of view but they couldn't understand mine
when we were placing him for adoption. Once we went to visit and our son was
out of the unit and on a regular floor. . . . When we arrived all the nurse said
was, "Didn't anyone call you and tell you?" That was all she said. I thought he
was dead. Luckily his doctor was there and said he was transferred.*

Ann

*Both my OB and pediatrician were great. My obstetrician told me not to hesi-
tate to call if I just needed to talk. My pediatrician never once charged me for an
office visit, just medicine, supplies, et cetera. He told me we had enough to face
in the future without facing financial problems also.*

Trudy

*The heart specialist was great. We told him we were thinking of adoption and
he said, "You do what you have to. I, too, have been through tragedy and anyone
who has been will understand. Pay no attention to those who judge you. They
just don't understand what they're talking about."*

Beth and Daniel

*In the beginning the medical personnel kept their distance. I felt that they only
approached us when necessary. After reading the records from the hospital on
Nina, I felt very frustrated and angry that some doctors could be so judgmental.*

Pam

*We felt the message from our doctors was that it wasn't a big deal; they made
light of the situation. It was as if they didn't want to acknowledge how very
different it was. It made me feel worse because I was feeling so bad about it.*

Rona

*My husband got mad at our pediatrician. She told us she had had an amnio-
centesis. Why would she have it if she didn't care if she had a child with Down
syndrome or not?*

Kathleen

*The social worker at the hospital was wonderful. She was probably the most
helpful and nonjudgmental of anyone working with us. She called us several*

times asking what she could do to be of help, arranged counseling for us with a woman who has continued to be supportive, and gave us information about services for the baby.

Joanne

Our pediatrician spent needless months trying to find out what the problem was by telling me I was another nervous first mother and "with an adopted child, you never know!" We sought a new pediatrician.

Julie

My OB team was of no help. The hospital was of no help. They could have and should have had more resources about options since I was directly asking them. The hospital should have provided us with a genetic counselor or grieving counselor that day. It was Friday evening and we were told to wait until Monday.

Randy and Dave

My pediatrician at the time should never have said she had never dealt with a problem such as ours—we felt like freaks.

Lexie

Our OB was supportive of our decision, but was surprised that adoption was even an option. Our pediatrician felt that we could do a good job of raising the baby, but was nonjudgmental when he found out we were placing him for adoption. The nursing staff assumed we would be taking the baby home, and, therefore, bent over backwards to get me to bond with him.

Mary Ann

Our geneticist was very helpful—he didn't give us any advice; he just stated the facts and told us where to go for help. I also remember him saying that he had known very devout Catholics who had said they would never consider having an abortion, then decided to terminate a troubled pregnancy. He'd also known others who were pro-choice but had decided to keep their genetically imperfect babies. This made me feel better, knowing that there were others out there struggling with the same decisions we were faced with and doing what they felt right for them despite their religious or moral convictions.

Barbara

None of our doctors were that involved with us. At birth, my OB said to me: "A child like this could break up a marriage, a family, and embarrass your older child's life." He never called me during my six-week recovery period to see how I was. He disappointed us.

Lauren

I was going through a clinic that specialized in high-risk pregnancy. Instead of seeing three to four doctors every visit, my doctor saw to it that I only had to see her. After Angela was born the social worker from the clinic spent hours talking to me and they had another lady from the hospital social service who spent hours with me. It would have been helpful for the hospital to have put me in contact with parents. Everyone I contacted and talked to was through my own efforts.

Cathie

The doctor taking care of my baby in the step-down nursery would always look me in the eyes and say, "How is Mom doing today?" He made me feel so guilty. He knew we were putting the baby up for adoption. But what is so bizarre, this doctor told our social worker that he had a lot of respect for us. He thought Louis and I were two of the most remarkable people he had ever met. He thought we were very courageous and gave us credit for really thinking about our decision. Why couldn't he tell us that?

Eileen

All of the doctors [at the hospital where the baby was] were most kind. They took time to talk to me on the phone, sometimes a few calls daily. They truly seemed to care about Emily and to be nonjudgmental towards me. The genetic counselor working with the doctor who tested Emily was helpful and informative.

Jan

FRIENDS

> The most helpful thing for someone to say in this case would be: "Gee, this must be a tough decision for you to make. I just want to let you know that whatever you decide to do is OK with me. I'll still be your friend. Let me know if I can be of any help."
>
> Barbara

The reactions of friends often surprise people who are in a crisis. Many families find truth in the adage, "You find out who your friends really are." It is often the person one least expects who will be the most supportive. Some parents do not hear from friends they would expect to because those friends just don't know what to say. Many people found support from new friends rather than from longtime friends. Beth and Dan learned from their experience, "Our friendships have more quality and are more satisfying than before. . . . Our circle of friends has grown smaller, but richer." Other families say that their circle of friends has grown larger through the new contacts they have made.

Close friends, like family, are grieving the loss, too. Sometimes they are *too* close to be of help and to be objective. Those who have never experienced a significant loss are seldom as supportive as those who have. In a state of dismay and vulnerability new parents often don't know what help for which to ask. Friends may want to do something to show they care, but don't know what to do to help. In answer to "What can I do?," the following suggestions are offered:

Bring a meal—most people in a state of grief don't feel like preparing meals; parents who had friends bring food greatly appreciated it.

Take the other children for a few hours—the time needed to talk and educate often takes time from the other children. It is good for those children to be in a family setting away from the turmoil. Parents need to have time away from their children to meet with and talk to other people and, more importantly, to each other.

Call—to check on the parents and don't be offended if they don't feel like talking.

Learn about the stages of grief—and be prepared for any kind of reaction from the parents. One of the most common reactions to the news is anger. Parents who are angry may unleash this anger on anyone who is nearby. They may be depressed and negative. Positive comments, such as "God wouldn't give you anything you can't handle" or "You're the perfect parents to raise a child like this," may *not* be appreciated, especially if the parents are considering an adoption plan.

If you don't know what to say, say so—some parents will want to hear you say you're sorry, others may be offended by this statement. Don't try to fill in the conversation with chatter. Usually just your presence is appreciated, but if you sense that the parents would rather be alone, ask them and accept their honesty.

Don't try to express your opinions to the parents—if you haven't "been there," you *don't* know what you would do.

Offer to take the baby for a few hours—and if possible, hold the baby when you are there. Be accepting of the baby's condition, but don't try to tell the parents of all the accomplishments this baby will attain unless you are knowledgeable about the disability.

Be prepared to listen and ask questions—if parents don't seem receptive to the questions, stop asking. Many parents need to talk, others want to make their decisions in solitude.

Parents Talk

Friends who were the most helpful "mourned" with us over an incredibly painful decision. . . . They listened to us, cried with us and I really felt so many of our close friends felt a tremendous amount of pain with us. One who was not helpful asked me, "Why can't you get strong enough to handle raising a child with Down syndrome when other people can handle it?" I really did not appreciate this, as she, my friend, couldn't possibly imagine the amount of pain my husband and I were in.

Mary

[The least helpful were friends who] kept saying they were sorry. I got extremely sick and tired of people telling me they were sorry.

Kevin

Friends or acquaintances who had tragedies of their own with the loss of a child contacted us. Their kind notes and conversations were comforting. One friend, in particular, had a child with a genetic birth defect and had placed her baby for adoption. She was very helpful.

Lauren and Michael

To be helpful to me at the intense moments was to just sit and listen to me talk. It seemed the more I talked, the more came out of me . . . my fears of not knowing if I could handle the baby. Friends pointed these things out when they really listened to me.

Eileen

Helpful—just being there and understanding. Unhelpful—acting as if there were no problem.

Max

Two friends of mine were super-supportive. They didn't "crowd," but their presence was constant. They called, invited us over, talked, listened, offered information and insight.

Rona

Several people at our church who were childbearing age were condemning. What we did was a real threat to their illusions about themselves. A single man who gave up his lifestyle to care for his 83-year-old mother and 51-year-old mentally retarded brother was particularly supportive. He heard about us and sought us out to befriend us and encourage us. Both he and his mother thought the adoption was wonderful and that we deserved a medal. He's become our best friend and support since the adoption.

Beth and Daniel

Friends can help by explaining to their children how fortunate they are to be healthy. Children can be so cruel. It is hard enough for a sibling to comprehend what is wrong with his sister or brother without having other children ridicule him and make demeaning remarks about his sister.

Pam

Two of our friends sent dinner to our house which was very much appreciated because we were going to and from the hospital almost every day for two months. Some family and friends called too often to see how things were going but offered no help whatsoever in our time of need. I feel they were just calling to be nosy. One very close friend of mine said, "Oh, how can you do that?" when she learned of our idea that we might give our baby up. She was sitting at home with a "normal" 3-month-old baby girl. I think she must have given it more thought, because from then on she was very supportive, but I did feel very bad when she made that comment.

Lorraine

Family helped most by listening to us. Friends helped with some respite and listening. Many cried with us and supported us in whatever mood we were in.

Lee and Julie

Most helpful were friends who let us talk and who asked questions. Least helpful were those who refused to talk about the situation.

Mary Ann and Hank

Friends came to visit and most offered to hold the baby and treated him like any other infant. I welcomed their warmth for him. . . . I remember how tired I was when people left (from putting up a front), but I know it did feel good to hear about "normal" life. . . . One woman called and honestly said, "I don't know what to say." Just the call, to show that she wasn't passing judgment on me, was helpful. Another friend told me how she had sat over her son's bed the night she heard about us and cried, thankful for his normalcy.

Joanne

Emily was in the hospital for a month. Jan's brother and some of our friends visited and held and fed Emily so she got extra attention in the nursery. Acting as our surrogates is a debt we shall never be able to repay.

Jeff

My friends and family were very helpful. They supported our decision. They kept their distance when we asked them to. They were close by when we needed them. They did practical things for us when we first returned home such as cooking, cleaning, laundry, et cetera.

Jan

I think the least helpful is when a friend or family member finds out that Nicole is still not talking, or that she is still in diapers, and proceeds to tell me about a friend of a friend who didn't talk till they were 4 years old or didn't potty train till 4½ and then just blossomed. This has no relevance to Nicole's situation.

Sue

It was most helpful for them to be there when I needed to talk. I spent three weeks back East at my sister's summer home by the beach the month after I got the amnio results. She paid for the groceries and gave me time alone with my girls. It helped to be with my family and gave me a break. I think I would have gone over the edge had I not had that time away from everything.

Cathie

Some friends and family supported me which was helpful. Some harassed me which made a difficult situation even worse.

Kathleen

What I didn't care for was unsolicited advice from well-meaning family and friends. If someone said I should get an abortion, I became defensive and angry; if they said everything would turn out just fine, I became worried and depressed ("How do you know?").

Barbara

The friends who helped the most were those who listened, listened, and listened, who were understanding of our decision, not necessarily accepting, but really making an effort to understand how difficult it all was. It was helpful to have friends and family offer information (e.g., names and numbers of people raising children with Down syndrome) but let us decide whether or not we wanted to use it. It was not helpful to be left alone by my good friends. I know it must have been uncomfortable for them, but I really needed them and many weren't there for me.

Randy

Note to New Parents

It is important for you to build a support system to help you through the grief and decision making. A counselor is usually necessary to serve as an unbiased party. When looking for a counselor, look for someone who listens to you, makes you feel comfortable, and seems trustworthy.

Search out the local parent support group and find someone from that group to whom you feel you can relate. If you feel that you are hearing too many "positives," it might be helpful to ask to talk with someone who is not so overly enthusiastic and who had similar initial feelings and can remember them.

If you feel angry with doctors or other professionals, ask yourself if your feelings are justified or if you are directing your frustration about the situation at those who delivered the news. Don't be afraid to search out other professionals if necessary.

Try to keep yourself surrounded by people who are supportive and avoid, when possible, those who are not. You probably don't want to hurt others' feelings, but you also need to protect yourself from people who may inadvertently hurt you. Try your best to keep those who are most supportive within reach and find a tactful way of getting time and space away from those who cause you to suffer more.

Don't be afraid to ask for specific help—it makes people feel good to help others and many people don't know what to do.

Direction

We long for God's green light,
An affirmation that our
   earthly struggles are
   in the right direction.
Our decisions seem
   to be made
   in a
   cloud of indecision.
We search for a sign,
   a burning bush,
   a cloud,
   a pillar of fire.
Yet answers come
   in strange ways.
A new perspective given
   by the words
   of a friend,
   mysterious circumstances.

Closed doors
   can become
   open doors.
Red lights
   can turn green.

Stop signs
   can say
   go ahead.

Only in retrospect
   can we see
   that through
   each trial,
   each decision,
   each turn in
      the road,
   our steps
   have been directed.

And when the
   impossible
   becomes
   beautifully possible,
   we are reassured
   of God's hand
      in
         our
            lives.

                              Kay Haggart Mills

4

Lonely Choices

ISOLATION

> I never felt so alone in my life. I had everyone with me but I was alone in my pain.
>
> Eileen

No amount of support can fully alleviate the sense of isolation that prevails for most new parents. Each parent must face his or her own moral and spiritual beliefs alone since few marriage partners have exactly the same spiritual or moral upbringing. Each individual must face his or her own limitations and accept those of their spouse. Family finances are usually personal concerns, problems shared only within the immediate family. Parents must face the repercussions their decision will cause within the nuclear family; either decision is sure to cause a disruption to their other children. Ultimately, the decision rests upon just the two people who will have to face the outcome of their decision. Only they will have to live inside themselves and inside their own home once the decision is final.

SPIRITUAL CONCERNS

> How could God do this to a precious angel like Hollie? I hated God for what he did to her life and ours. Life had so much joy and He took it away.
>
> Julie

Parents who give birth to a child with a disability often hear over and over again "God has given you a special gift," or "God wouldn't give you anything you can't handle." These words can be very painful for parents who are considering an adoption plan for a child with a disability. Many parents don't want the "gift" God had given them. Beth felt, "If God was giving gifts, he must have made a big mistake and delivered it to the wrong house." Mary Ann and Hank found it difficult to respond to these statements and were always wondering if these people would be so sure of themselves if God had "chosen" them for this wonderful "gift." The guilt most parents feel for considering adoption is only enhanced by these well-meaning people. After all, if *God* has given us this "special gift," who are *we* to give it away?

Barbara, the mother of three children, two with disabilities, shared her opinion of these words:

Euphemisms such as these discourage parents of handicapped children from being honest about how they feel. There are times that we resent our children for tying us down, for making us work harder, for having to be lifelong nurturers. . . . Sure, there are times when life seems great and you feel blessed to share your love with this special child, but there are also times when it doesn't seem as if it could get much worse!

Some parents, like Kathleen, feel that God is punishing them for some wrongdoing: "I still believe in God and love Him, but I can't understand why He did this to me or allowed nature to do this to me. I thought He might be getting back at me for the few things I did wrong in my life." People would say to Pam, "God is testing you" or "He has a reason." She would reply, "Why?"

Some parents do find that faith carries them through the decision-making process. Mary Ann, who initially felt she was being punished, "later began to feel that God had nothing to do with our child having Down syndrome, but God did help us make the ultimate decision which was best for us, our family, and the baby." Other parents lose their faith. Pam and Richard are both Catholic. Pam stated: "I have lost most of my faith since my daughter's birth. I just could not understand how God or anyone else would let children be born with different handicaps or illnesses in which they suffer."

Some parents are fearful of calling their minister, rabbi, or priest. They seem to think that these people will judge them. Those who have talked with clergy people usually have found very positive support. Most large hospitals are staffed with chaplains from several faiths who are very experienced in dealing with grief and loss. A chaplain usually will talk with parents even if they've already been released from the hospital.

Parents Talk

When tragedies happen, we want to blame God. We did at first, but He is not to blame. We searched out Rabbi Kushner who wrote When Bad Things Happen to Good People. *He helped us to realize that "he may not be the wrong child, but you may be the wrong parents for this child." . . . Rabbi Kushner also helped us to believe that God didn't make this happen, nature did and God is here to give us support to get through this.*

Lauren and Michael

I question God after going through this. I know my own capabilities, whether God feels I can handle more or not. I've only got one life and I have to make the decisions to make that life the best, not God nor anyone else.

Trudy

I feel that my prayers were answered by finding a loving family to accept and love a child that I emotionally was unable to accept. In my heart I feel the decision was best.

Warren

The more I heard how "God had given me this special gift" the more guilt I felt and the more pressure to live up to that image. I wished He'd given the gift to them or to anyone else. . . . When we asked unbelievingly and fearfully for His help, He opened the gates of heaven and poured His love, His grace, and understanding on us and gave us Stephanie [the adoptive mom]. I have never felt condemnation from Him, only love.

Beth

The world was a different place before we got the news [about Hollie's disabilities]. I haven't seen much of the old one since. I have some faith back because we have been given the strength to survive and because we found a good family for our child.

Lee

I began believing it [God wouldn't give you anything you can't handle], that it was my, our, fate and yet inside I was overwhelmed! Many times I found myself thinking it, too, but knew I was so unprepared and so unequipped to deal with it.

Julie

I remember thinking, and still feel, that people said that to me ["God wouldn't give you anything you can't handle"] because of lack of anything else to say, because they were at a loss for words and didn't know how to comfort me. I do believe and feel strongly that under all the "rare circumstances" of our son's "shaky birth" and serious conditions at birth, the fact that he survived and pulled through meant that God wanted him to make it, and because he came from my husband and me we had the responsibility of raising him.

Mary

I felt angry when people said those words. I saw nothing special about caring for a child for all the days of my life. I felt that God must be losing his vision. I thought, "He knows that I teach children with severe behavior problems, why would He add to that? Aren't I doing my fair share?" Usually, in response, I'd say nothing but I think at times we responded with, "We don't agree with that," and after a while I almost anticipated people making those kind of comments and so would beat them to the punch and tell them how angry I was at people saying such crap.

Randy

One of my biggest fears of giving up Brian, our "imperfect" child, was that God would punish me by causing something bad to happen to my "perfect" child. I finally sought out the hospital chaplain. He helped me to realize that perhaps what God had meant for me to handle was the painful "letting go," and that adoption was a loving choice, not one for which I should be punished.

Joanne

I cringe every time someone makes a statement about God's special gift. What kind of statement is this to see a child suffer throughout its life?

Pam

If God didn't give people things they couldn't handle, then why are people having nervous breakdowns, becoming alcoholics or drug addicts? Some of them can't handle reality, and couldn't handle what God gave them. This special gift was a heartache for me. Who would want to be that special?

Kathleen

I went to see a priest who was a comfort. He told me we are all God's children. I gave birth but this does not mean I have to raise my baby. He told me that maybe God did choose Louis and I to have this baby knowing we would make the right and fair decision for the baby.

I guess when it is time for all men and women to stand up and be judged by God I will be holding my baby's hand along with her adoptive Mom. She has two mommies—one loving and raising her and the other loving and praying for her.

Eileen

We felt like those who made those comments were giving us only one course of action. The implication was "Do it this way or your soul is lost."

Mary Ann and Hank

For a time my beliefs and faith were somewhat shattered. I desperately needed God to help me through this, but part of me turned away from Him. . . . I was angry not only for myself, but for what my children were going through. They'd been through enough.

Cathie

Sometimes these euphemisms ["God gives special children to special parents," etc.] make me feel good and special, like I was chosen by some higher power to be the parent of this handicapped child. . . . But there were (and still are) times when I felt that I was not "worthy" of such an honor—when I lose my temper, am impatient with my children, and get depressed or feel sorry for myself. Say-

ings such as these tend to make me feel guilty if I don't live up to the image portrayed.

Barbara

We are existentialist atheists. We have always believed that many things happen by chance without design or reason. This just confirmed this belief, and, for a while, we were more acutely aware that the way we cope with life, by operating as if everything is going to be OK, is really not a sure thing. Anything could happen to us. It's not a comforting thought, but true, nonetheless.

Jan and Jeff

I have prayed more since Nicole was born than I ever have in my life; first, praying that she would turn normal, and, of course, asking, "Why me?" I was very angry with God, but now I realize he is the one who gave Rick and me the strength to follow through on adoption.

Sue

I asked people to leave God out of this, or, if I felt like talking, I said God gave me a child which I should give to someone else who was meant to care for such a child. God has given me mental anguish that I have to deal with for the rest of my life. There is really no good that has come out of this at all! During this time I lost all my faith in God and was very saddened by this. How could God create a child with no hope? How could God do this to me, us? Once I changed my spiritual understanding of God and faith with the help of the book When Bad Things Happen to Good People *I was able to cope.*

Lexie

I talked to our rabbi and he didn't know what to say. He's young and not married, but shared that he had had a dog and it died so he knew loss. I spoke to him two or three times and he was very interested in listening but I felt I was enhancing his experience.

Rona

This presupposes a belief in a certain kind of God, one that is like a person who can see everything and who, with a whisk of his hand, can alter the affairs on Earth or anywhere else. This is a setup for disappointment and anger at God because many prayers will go unanswered. If the spiritual void must be filled with a god, let it be a god from within to whom you pray for the strength to cope with whatever may befall you. . . . What happened to us was a matter of chance (1 in 50,000). My spirituality guides my actions and my responses but not what happens to me.

Max

FINANCES AND SUPPORT SERVICES

Nina's medical bills were exceeding the insurance coverage we had. Soon after Nina was born we went bankrupt. The bills just kept coming and they were very demanding. If she were placed in the developmental center family placement program she would be eligible for Medicaid and SSI.

Pam

The financial circumstances of the families interviewed for this book ranged from a single mother receiving child support and disability to a couple who are both medical professionals and financially secure. Although most families considered their financial status, finances were seldom a primary reason for choosing adoption. The welfare of the child and the rest of the family was foremost in the minds of all couples interviewed. For some, like Pam and Richard, the financial security of the family played a major role in their decision, yet, in spite of the bills, they may not have chosen alternative care if they felt Nina was capable of recognizing them. Pam says: "First we thought of Nina and what type of medical care she needed. We thought of our family, what it was doing to us, how it would affect our son. . . . Nina did not know who we were. If she did know I do not think I could have placed her in family care."

Finances often play a less direct part in the decision-making process. For Joanne, there was no possible way to quit her job and keep the family financially stable: "It was such a dilemma. I felt I would have to quit my job to give Brian the best care possible but quitting my job would mean cutting our income by two-thirds. My husband's job was temporary with no medical benefits. We had just bought our first home. It all seemed so overwhelming."

For Kevin and Ann, providing the necessary care for Michael would have meant traveling nearly 100 miles to a large medical center several times a week. Not only would this have been a financial drain because Ann would not have been able to work, there would be traveling expenses and child-care expenses for their other son. In addition to the financial worries there would be a physical and emotional drain on the parent doing the traveling.

Some states may provide stipends for adoptive parents and not for birthparents, forcing some parents into considering adoption so that their child will have more financial provisions. Cathie worried continually that her limited income would not allow her to provide Angela with the proper care and was extremely upset over the unfairness of this policy: "I applied for medical assistance but because I have equity in my house, Angela doesn't qualify. This is a real sore spot because families who adopt special needs children get a government subsidy and free medical. It's like a slap in the face to the birthparents." In spite of this, her final decision was to raise her daughter. She has since fought for state funded programs for children like Angela and also has been approved for assistance. In fact, if the family meets the income criteria, eligibility for benefits for Supplemental Security Income (SSI) is now determined for babies with some disabilities, including Down syndrome, as soon as a diagnosis is made. Birth *or* adoptive families may qualify depending upon their income. Medicaid benefits are determined at local levels and will therefore differ from state to state or, sometimes, within a state. Often children in foster care will be eligible for Medicaid, but will not be eligible if adopted, thereby discouraging foster parents from adopting a child.

Other programs to help birth and/or adoptive parents pay medical bills do exist in some locations. Brian's physical therapy was not covered by the medical insurance provided by Joanne's employer, yet when she investigated programs she learned that this part of his care would be covered by a state program for children with disabilities. There was even a program that would pay for respite care for Brian for a specified number of hours per year. Programs do exist, but are different in different localities.

The availability of resources and programs also may play a part in the adoption decision. Families who live in areas where resources are not readily available may consider it best for their child to live in a locality where services are more easily accessed. However, before making the decision based on the lack of resources, parents should investigate what programs are provided. Some states have visiting professionals who travel to rural localities. Parents need to search out the resources available.

Candid examination of personal strengths and limitations will help parents judge their own ability to cope financially and logistically to meet the needs of their child.

HOW LONG TO MAKE THE DECISION?

> We searched within and without. We knew the decision we had to make had to be made soon, but I could not see any serious decision making until the deep depression cleared.
>
> Max

Most parents will be in a state of grief or "shock" for several days or weeks. The decision-making process can be extremely draining and parents often feel physically and emotionally exhausted. In cases where the diagnosis is made at birth, the mother will be recuperating from childbirth, sometimes from surgery. If the diagnosis is prenatal, there will be time restraints that parents of newborns do not need to worry about.

Parents often express feeling as if they are caught up in a "time warp." Days may seem extremely long. An event that took place yesterday may seem as if it happened a year ago. Yet, conversely, an event that happened a few days before may seem as if it was only moments earlier. For many parents, this feeling of a "time warp" may last for months.

Many parents who continued with the decision-making process worried about the amount of time it was taking to make a decision. "How long is 'too long' for the benefit of the baby?" they would ask. Many didn't feel themselves forming an attachment as they might have with a "normal" baby, perhaps because they wanted to protect themselves from the painful "letting go" if that were to be the chosen path. They worried that their child wouldn't form a close attachment with a new mother, or with any mother, if adopted "too late." One family's pediatrician advised, "Newborns only need consistent care by a warm, loving person. It's more important that you make a decision you can live with." Rick and Mary advise, "It took us six months to get over the grief and realize that our son could bring us joy."

Several other families experienced frustration over the "red tape" encountered in the adoption process. Randy and Dave's son, Jake, was in respite for four weeks, much longer than they expected. "We felt frustrated and angry at the system and at people who led us to believe they knew what they were doing. We wanted Jake placed earlier than that so he could begin bonding with his new family."

Another concern is the availability of parents to adopt babies who are several weeks, or months, old. Janet Marchese of the National Down Syndrome Adoption Exchange advises that children with Down syndrome are adoptable at "6 weeks, 6 months, or even 6 years." The younger the child, the easier it is to find a family, but there are families willing to adopt children of almost any age.

The decision should not be rushed, but living with the ambiguity of indecision is very stressful for the entire family. All families who have lived through this decision-making process agree that once a decision is made, it is easier to pick up the pieces and go on. It is important to consider both the availability of adoptive parents and "bonding" between the baby and his new family. But, it is equally important that parents are confident of their choice. They must be able to live with the decision once it is made.

THE FINAL DECISION

> I knew from the day he was born that I couldn't keep him but I kept my pain buried, even from my husband. . . . I knew that I could not give him the unconditional love he deserved without having the guilt of being his natural parent.
>
> Trudy

One of the questions that new parents typically ask is, "How did you make your final decision?" Many people kept hoping that the decision would be clear, that the answer would magically appear. Not many parents have God show up before them to tell them what to do. It is important to remember that no one can give the parents an answer.

Though there is seldom a black or white answer, most parents feel a peaceful resolve at some point. Some parents, like Trudy, quoted earlier, have an initial feeling ·hat stays with them continually, even as they educate themselves. Most indicate leaning more one way than the other, and as they educate themselves they feel a stronger pull in one direction. Some parents will just "know" that the decision is right for them at some point in the process. After Lanier had been in foster care for a few days Mary decided, "To place my son would have been an unbearable choice; the guilt would have 'eaten me alive' . . . wondering if he was well, being stimulated enough, if he had gotten to sit on Santa's knee . . . if his mommy was there to comfort him like I would if he woke up from a bad dream." Cathie and Joanne had similar experiences, yet their final decisions were different. Cathie remembered crying over her baby saying, "You're not going anywhere." Joanne had her son home for an afternoon while he was in foster care and spoke aloud to him, "You're going to have a new mommy and daddy who will love you a whole lot." Both remembered their words as being totally spontaneous, yet neither made the *conscious* decision for several more weeks.

Families who have lived through this recommend that parents find what makes them feel most at peace with themselves. Cathie advises, "In this heart-wrenching decision, everyone has to do what they feel at peace inside with, whether it be to give your child up for adoption or to keep your child."

Most parents who have struggled with this decision, who have educated themselves and looked at their lives realistically, have few regrets. In spite of the resolve, most parents, especially those who choose adoption, also experience days or moments of questioning, of wondering "what if I'd made the other decision." They learn to live with this ambivalence and it becomes a part of their lives.

Parents Talk

We went to the library and took out books about Down syndrome. . . . The book A Difference in the Family *sort of confirmed our decision, but we had to see a child with Down syndrome before we could make our final decision. We visited a family with a 3-year-old child with Down syndrome. The parents greeted us with open arms which we appreciated very much. When we left their house we both knew we couldn't do it. The child demanded so much attention and it was very obvious that his younger brother did not get the attention that he needed. We felt so sorry for all of them. We didn't want our 2-year-old son to suffer from lack of attention because we knew we would devote so much time to our daughter.*

Lorraine and Warren

The bottom line is we were unable to cope. . . . I had been depressed to one degree or another for the past three-and-a-half years. I was having these horrible thoughts on a daily basis. Every morning I wished that she didn't come out of her bedroom—that I would go in and find her dead. Or that she would die in a car accident, or drown in a pool. Although I've never thought of killing her myself, my husband and I both had wished that they had never revived her at birth. We had never expressed that thought to each other till recently. . . . When I could no longer stand the pain, I discussed it with Rick and the following day made that first very difficult phone call to an adoption agency.

Sue

I agonized over keeping her, was it the best for her? I was so afraid of making the wrong decision for her sake. What if I failed? She would be the one to suffer. Now, looking back, all the talking, all the reading and having her home helped me in my final decision. From July 8 [when I got the amnio results] until I made my final decision there wasn't a day that I didn't cry. I've never felt such pain and heartache. . . . The week before Christmas I was holding Angela and crying and I said out loud, "You're not going anywhere" and for the first time since July 8 I felt at peace. It was another month before I actually made the decision [to raise her myself].

Cathie

I kept hoping that God would give me a sign. I prayed more than I ever had in my entire life. I didn't make my final decision until I met the adoptive parents, and even then I struggled with my ambivalence. I wasn't sure that I could go through with the signing of the papers until the day I signed them. I signed them only because I knew that there were special people waiting to hear that they would be the parents of my son and that they were thrilled with the prospect of parenting him. I was devastated.

Joanne

We had a clear knowledge of our limitations. The pregnancy was not planned. We had two kids and felt maxed out with them. . . . We felt that caring for a child with Down syndrome, one who had not even been planned, could be a real danger to our marriage and potentially very destructive to our family unit.

Beth and Daniel

We searched our souls. We felt unable to raise and care for a special needs child, especially one with an unknown prognosis. We felt too "old" (we're both in our 40s) to care for her for her lifetime and knew we didn't have the emotional equipment for the long-term care she needed. Our final decision was based on our love for her and for her well-being.

Lee and Julie

We listened to our hearts and to our own peace of mind. We brought Lanier home.

Mary and Rick

I visited people who had a 6-year-old girl who has Down syndrome and she was on the same level as my 18-month-old daughter. I knew if I saw that every day it would break my heart. I knew that no matter what I sacrificed that I couldn't make my baby "better." I just wouldn't have been a good mother for her.

Kathleen

We think that, short of raising our son, we did as much as we thought possible. We talked mostly to parents raising children with Down syndrome, read everything we could get our hands on, met families, went to a support group outing, counseled with a psychologist, met with a physician from a developmental clinic who specializes in Down syndrome, visited a preschool which serves children with developmental delays, began early infant stimulation classes with Jake, talked to others who had considered adoption but didn't, talked with others who chose adoption, spoke to an adoptive family, and spoke to the family who wanted to adopt Jake. We also talked to a school psychologist of thirty years who was straightforward in sharing experiences and information about families who were raising children with Down syndrome. She basically confirmed all that we had feared.

Randy and Dave

We spent a lot of time educating ourselves, reading, talking to parents, talking to professionals, . . . talking to our priest, our families, to each other and praying. We feared that keeping him would create stress that would destroy our family unit, that life with a child with Down syndrome would be such a burden that our other children would suffer, and that we couldn't give him proper care. Our extended families live so far away that we would have had no family support in the care of this child.

Mary Ann and Hank

We did a great deal of reading. We were visited by and we visited children with achondroplasia and their parents. We tried to base our decision on what we thought would be the best for the child, our other children, and ourselves, and we helped another family by the way.

Max

I will never forget the words of the adoption coordinator from Little People of America who called from Texas. She said to me in her Texan drawl: "Honey, if you can't just give that child a stool to kick around so she can reach things, and otherwise treat her just the same as all your other children, then let someone else do the job. Don't feel bad about it forever, just let someone else do the job." And she was right. We felt that a family that could provide for her psychological and social needs was better for her, but if we hadn't found an appropriate family we would have raised her ourselves. We came to terms with our own limitations. We just couldn't do the job [of raising Naomi] as well as the adoptive family we chose.

                                                                              Rona

The loss of our dreams and fantasies of parenting a healthy, normal Emily was too great. We feared we would regret having her and she would sense this in our parenting. We want so much for her to be happy and feel good about herself. I knew it would be almost impossible for my feelings of loss, regret, guilt, et cetera, not to come across and . . . this would just not be fair for her.

                                                                              Jeff

Simultaneously, my husband and I realized very clearly and powerfully that there was no way we could or should raise Emily. I was lying in bed, in the hospital, trying to imagine how we would cope and suddenly, like a flash, I thought, "Who am I kidding? There is just no way in hell I am up to this job; no matter how much I love and adore my child, it won't be enough to stop me from feeling trapped, angry, and resentful. This can't work. It will hurt me, our marriage, and our child." Just as I thought this, Jeff took my hands in his and said, "Jan, we're both atheists and we don't think there is any God who wants us to raise this child. I don't think we should keep Emily. I think we should give her up for adoption." She was 2 days old and although the pain of separating from her was extended and agonizing and indeed is still in progress, we never even considered changing our minds.

                                                                              Jan

We considered as many options as we could think of—abortion, adoption, institutionalization, and finally having and keeping the baby. . . . I kept thinking about my other child with LMBBS. We had no way of knowing that he would be born with a genetic condition. We were not faced with a choice on whether to have him or not. He was just born to us and we had to muddle our way through finding out what was wrong with him and how to best care for him. I'm not saying it was easy. There were many days that I would have traded him in for a "normal, healthy" child, but it was never so bad that I wished that he hadn't been born. . . .

At that time I was president of a LMBBS support network and I kept thinking that the person who would adopt this baby would probably want to join our network and I would be in the awkward position of giving these people advice on raising their (really my) child. That seemed ludicrous. I think it was at this point that I abandoned all thoughts of adoption and went full steam ahead with plans to keep this baby, love her, and if worse came to worse, reconsider these other options (institutionalization, foster care, adoption) later.

                                                                          Barbara

My pediatrician was trying to be patient, but it showed that she was getting tired and inconvenienced with going to the hospital every day. She called me to encourage me to come to a decision and said, "Every baby is cute, and every baby is needy, but she needs to be held by a 'caregiver' and you should make up your minds soon." I was hurt by her words but I knew how true they were. We made our minds up [chose adoption] shortly after that.

Lexie

We wanted 100 percent for our baby. We weren't sure that we were the right people to help her grow. We knew if we brought her home it would be like a funeral, curtains drawn, hiding our pain, sheltering her, but not helping her. We probably could have given her 60 percent—not good enough. We knew the adoptive family would give her 100 percent. They both have degrees in special education, but more importantly they could look at her objectively. When I looked at her my heart was on the table. She needed attention now—I was still in a fog.

Eileen

I thought I'd feel sorry for the baby everyday, every time I looked at her. It would hurt me to see her suffer. We tried to look through each other's fears and help each other see what we could not admit to ourselves.

Louis

I based my decision on what I thought was best for Michael. I read some literature that the hospital gave me. I listened and thought about what the doctors had told me. After doing this I realized that I couldn't give Michael what he needed. . . . After admitting and accepting the fact that I couldn't handle it, and then learning that there were people that could care for Michael and give him what he needed, my decision seemed easier to live with. I didn't feel like such a failure.

Kevin

My husband said there was no way that he could care for a baby that would need everything that our son would need. Also, doctors said in some cases where there are other children involved their learning may suffer to a point where they would be a slow learner. To keep my second son I would lose the man that I love very much and a son that's most of my life. I couldn't lose or hurt either of them so I chose to hurt myself [by choosing adoption for Michael].

Ann

We talked to other families, bought and read books, spoke with Rabbi Kushner. . . . Our final decision was made when we visited a family with a 6-year-old girl with Down syndrome and realized that having Down syndrome isn't just delayed or being slower than norm but being retarded. She acted 2 and was considered average for Down syndrome. We also visited the social worker in charge of the Down Syndrome Clinic and spoke to parents at the clinic about the pros and cons of keeping such a child. . . . I realized that this wasn't for me.

Lauren

Note to New Parents _____

The decision to make an adoption plan for your baby should not be made quickly or while still in a state of confusion and "shock." It is helpful to consider that you may not be living in the same time reference that you do under "normal" life circumstances. An hour can seem like a day, a day like a week. Take the time *you* need to make careful decisions. The adoption decision is irreversible.

You are the only people who will have to live with your final decision. When you close the door to your home, you are the ones who will be facing yourselves and your decision for the rest of your lives. You probably will need to ask yourselves which decision will be *less* painful. Choosing other parents to raise your child will not make the pain go away. You should not look at adoption as a "way out" or a way to go back in time. You must think instead of moving forward, of building a new life.

And a woman who held a babe against
her bosom said, Speak to us of Children.
   And he said:
   Your children are not your children.
   They are the sons and daughters of Life's
longing for itself.
   They come through you but not from
you,
   And though they are with you yet they
belong not to you.

   You may give them your love but not
your thoughts,
   For they have their own thoughts.
   You may house their bodies but not
their souls,
   For their souls dwell in the house of to-
morrow, which you cannot visit, not even
in your dreams.
   You may strive to be like them, but seek
not to make them like you.
   For life goes not backward nor tarries
with yesterday.

   You are the bows from which your children as living arrows are sent forth.
   The archer sees the mark upon the path
of the infinite, and He bends you with His
might that His arrows may go swift and far.
   Let your bending in the archer's hand
be for gladness;
   For even as He loves the arrow that flies,
so He loves also the bow that is stable.

from The Prophet
by Kahlil Gibran

5

Family Issues:
Before, During, and After
the Decision

EXTENDED FAMILY

> My father's exact words: "Matthew is my grandson and I love him,
> but you are my daughter and you come first."
>
> Trudy

Extended family members often can be the best support, or, in some cases, worst enemies. Other family members will also grieve the loss of the baby that was expected; some will feel pain for the new parents.

Many parents end up educating extended family members at the same time they educate themselves. Some family members may be open to receive the information and others, in their state of grief, may deny that there is any problem and refuse information. Most people know their families well enough that responses are fairly predictable.

Many parents experience the problem of having someone in one of their extended families offer to raise the baby for them. Usually a sister, sometimes a mother, makes this offer. It hurts deeply to have someone to whom one is close say, in essence, "I can do it even though you can't." The offers to take the baby are a way of gaining control over a situation in which they have no control. It tends to be a coping mechanism for them; by taking the baby they can prevent *their* loss and most of them truly believe that they are helping the parents.

Opinions often are implied rather than expressed, although many parents have had family members tell them bluntly what they "should" do. In a state of vulnerability it is easy to misinterpret actions of others. Many parents interviewed felt judged by some family members.

Several families made use of telephone answering machines during the decision-making process, to screen out calls that might have been hurtful, but to still receive those much needed calls from people who were most understanding.

Parents Talk

Both of our families were very supportive of our decision. They felt the pain, too, and seemed to believe we were making the correct decision for ourselves. My father helped to put things in perspective for us because our heads were so foggy and confused. My parents helped, too, by having us to dinner often and by watching our son every day.

Lorraine

You find out when going through something like this how important family is. They asked if they helped more, would I consider keeping him, but they could go home at night and sleep in their own beds. I had to get up the next morning and face another day with no end in sight.

Trudy

Our families were all supportive of whatever decision we made; however, we know that many of them knew what they wanted us to do, but they really didn't pressure us.

Mary and Rick

It was our decision. My father made a very wise comment: "Everybody goes home and you're the ones who have to live with this when you shut the door." We are the ones who had to live with this child.

Lauren

We felt a couple members "judging" us in subtle ways. The main difficulty was when both Dave's sister and my sister volunteered to adopt Jake. That shocked us and we couldn't help but wonder how supportive they really were. We knew that they saw Jake only as he appeared—a sweet little baby to love—and that they couldn't see beyond that.

Randy

I have told only my sister what we are doing. She is very supportive and understanding. We are not going to tell the rest of the family until we get further into the adoption process. I think my mother will be the hardest hit. She has been in complete denial since Nicole was born.

Sue

Most of my family supported our decision. A couple, my mother and younger sister, just couldn't understand why we did what we did. They both started to run Ann down and blame her for Michael's problems. I don't talk to either of them anymore. They are not welcome anywhere near me or my family.

Kevin

We had no problem initially with our families. They supported our decision and still do, but they now don't want to talk about it. Many of them seem to feel that not talking about what happened or how we were coping was the best way to put it all behind us. We were desperate to have more children and scared to death that we wouldn't be able to or would have another child with Down syndrome. Many family members didn't seem very understanding of our anxiety.

Mary Ann and Hank

One of my sisters turned me in to the Department of Social Services because I would not let her adopt the baby. My mother and one sister supported me very much. They talked to people and found out about the heartache and they learned not to be judgmental. No one knows what something is like until it happens to them or what they would do in a certain situation. Now, one sister talks to me and three others don't.

Kathleen

All in all my friends and family were supportive, but no one really talked about how I was feeling. Everyone was afraid to discuss things with me because I was so depressed.

Just recently I had a confrontation with my sister who after five years told me she didn't agree with my decision nor does she agree with my values. This after five years of acceptance has come back to haunt me.

Lexie

My mother died of cancer before our decision was made and my family members were grieving her loss. . . . A lot of support came from my two nieces; one searched out information about Down syndrome and adoption for me, the other listened and listened without being judgmental. Overall the whole family has been accepting of our decision, although I don't think they understand the extent of our pain, how incredibly exhausting the whole process was, or the length of time it takes to recover from the grief.

Joanne

Family members seemed to disappear. Relationships were strained. My oldest brother and his wife did not approve of what we did. This made it difficult to be warm and open with them. . . . My younger brother even tried to talk me out of it. My youngest brother was my support. My parents, especially my father agreed with our decision, but they weren't available for emotional support.

Max

My Mom wanted to adopt the baby. She's 70 years old! What would happen ten or fifteen years from now? Louis's sister told us she was dead set against adoption. My sisters and brothers understood or tried to. Our parents went with us to visit schools—the baby was their granddaughter—they wanted to see for themselves. My father-in-law was so involved, so caring. They didn't try to influence us, just help us.

Eileen

My mother, sister, Lee's grandmother, close friends, and our social worker were very supportive. Hollie was the only grandchild and we both have small families. Lee's grandmother died a week after Hollie went to live with the adoptive family. We were very close to her and the dual losses were difficult.

Julie

I knew that my family actually wanted me to give Emily up, although they mourned her loss deeply. Three or four years previously, when one of their friend's children had a child born with Down syndrome, my parents asked me to consider amniocentesis when I became pregnant because they would not want me to have to raise a disabled child.

Jan

After we told my family about the decision, they asked if we were sure. For some reason both family, some friends, and agencies seem to think that the parents are too overwhelmed to know what they want or to be sure about it. The tendency to treat us like children, i.e., "Have you done your homework?," "Do you really want to do this?," et cetera, was both infuriating and guilt-inducing.

Jeff

My mother was very helpful and comforting. She kept by my side throughout this whole ordeal. If it were not for her, I don't know what I would have done.

I would say that the majority of the relatives were no help whatsoever. They kept their distance. A couple of family members made ignorant remarks or statements. I don't know if others didn't know what to say to us, or if they didn't understand what was happening.

Pam

I have six sisters and one brother so I had a lot of support. They were very supportive of adoption because they didn't feel I could raise Angela because of my medical problems and because I was always considered the "weak" one in our family. They opposed my raising Angela and when I decided to keep her I basically lost some family members' support. A lot of support seemed to be there as long as I did what they felt I should do. Others were there no matter what. My mother was super. She listened and prayed for me and she encouraged me to do what I felt was best. She never tried to sway me one way or the other.

Cathie

I confided in my sister that I was pregnant and knew the baby had the same syndrome as my son. She was very supportive, stating that it was our decision and that we would be the ones who would have to live with it. . . . After the initial shock, both of our mothers were very supportive. Other family members were sympathetic and supportive in their own way. I'm sure words were said behind our backs about our decision to have another handicapped child, but no one actually came out and said anything negative to us.

Barbara

My parents were supportive of us raising Rachel and wished they were closer. My brother has a severely retarded daughter, now in a state institution, so they'd been through this. My dad was real logical about our adoption decision, although I think a little upset: "What will people—our friends—think?" My mom felt sorry for Rachel. I told her "Rachel's in the best situation ever. You should feel sorry for us!"

My sister was pregnant with her third child and scared she was next in line for a retarded child. She said she would raise her Down syndrome child (if she had one) and wasn't supportive, but I knew she was really scared and what we did threatened her ideal of a perfect mother. She gave birth to a normal, healthy boy and cried in relief for a half-hour. She's now able to talk about it and her fears. I assured her I understood.

Beth

SIBLINGS

> I worried what effect two handicapped siblings would have on my oldest, nonhandicapped child. Would he be ashamed to have friends over to our house? Would he feel like the "odd man out"?
>
> Barbara

Most parents are very concerned about the effect a sibling with a disability will have on their other "normal" children or their future children. Some of the books about, and for, siblings of children with disabilities are listed in the appendix. Other families who are raising children with disabilities can provide insight to sibling relationships. Recently, family support groups have been trying to incorporate support systems for the siblings in the family. Two sibling support groups are listed in the appendix.

Many of the attitudes siblings have toward their brother or sister with the disability are reflections of the parental attitudes. Cathie initially considered adoption, but chose to raise Angela, who has Down syndrome. Angela's 12-year-old sister wrote an essay about Angela. An excerpt from this essay reflects the family attitude about Angela: "She's the 'wind beneath my wings,' so to say. I love her more than life itself and anyone who knows her is sure to say the same."

Parents who are considering adoption become very concerned about how to explain this choice to their other children, even those who may not be born yet. It is advisable for parents to have continued contact with a family doctor, pediatrician, or child psychologist or psychiatrist—someone who can answer questions for the parents and for the children as the children grow through different developmental stages.

Siblings in families who have chosen an adoption plan may experience feelings of insecurity. They will need constant reassurance that they *did not cause, do not have,* and *cannot get* the condition causing the disability.

They also need reassurance that they had nothing to do with the adoption. They will need to hear that if "something happens" to them—for example, if they get sick—that their parents won't send them off to live with someone else. In most instances the same questions will need to be answered over and over again, with constant explanations and reassurance.

Children of varying ages and with different personalities will react differently to the disappearance of the baby. If their brother or sister had been home, they may question, "What happened to the baby?" Children often experience sibling rivalry, which creates feelings of hostility toward a new baby. They may wish the baby gone. When that happens they may feel that they made the baby disappear. They will need constant reassurance that they did not play a part in the decision.

Most parents answer the same questions over and over again. It's important to be patient and to give information clearly and accurately. The questions may differ and the level of understanding will change as children grow through developmental stages. Many parents have decided to incorporate the decision into their family in an open, honest manner. Questions that are raised about the baby are freely answered. Most parents share any information they have about the baby's well-being with their other children.

Parents usually question when to tell those children who are too young to understand or remember, or the children not yet born, about the missing sibling. It is important that parents tell the children before they hear it from another source. If parents withhold information of this sort and the child hears it from another friend or relative, it can create feelings of hostility and destroy an element of trust. Again, a caring professional can help parents decide upon an appropriate time to share information about the sibling who was adopted.

Parents Talk

My daughter was only 3, but one day she asked if she were going to live with another family. I responded, "Oh, no, honey, you'll live with Mommy and Daddy forever."

Her confusion was evident with the kinds of questions she asked. One day she asked very bluntly, "Is my baby brother ever going to come back?" and the pain for me was incredible. I began with the long explanation, "Your brother has Down syndrome and he lives with another family who will give him the special care he needs," et cetera, when she remarked on the "doggy" in the car next to us. The ability to unexpectedly ask and then to shut off the conversation so quickly always amazes me.

About a year later we were talking about babies and she said, "We had a baby, but we sold him." As painful as it is for me, I try to explain again and again as honestly as I can, hoping that one day she will understand.

Joanne

Our children were upset and missed our son those ten days he was away with the adoptive family. They were all surprised when he was brought home and every day since then have showered him with love, affection, and constant stimulation. At that time my older girls were 8 and 5 and my son 4. They really wanted their baby brother home and I think I learned an important lesson from them: You just love the special child for who he is—just plain love—and you treat him like one of the others, just normally. You don't get caught up in the dilemma of what will this child be able to do or what he won't do, you just love him for the baby he is, a baby like all the rest, just one that needs a little more patience and extra help in achieving goals.

Mary

My son was young at the time, but now that he is 7, I answer all his questions as best as I can. I tried to explain that there were people who knew how to handle Matthew's special needs better than I could, but that it didn't mean that I didn't love Matthew. He hasn't really questioned what we've told him. He asks questions more about the Down syndrome than about the adoption. My two youngest are too young yet to question anything. In time, they will ask, and I will answer as honestly as I can. I am not ashamed of my decision and hope my other children will understand that.

Trudy

Lindsay, now 4, does not know about adoption. She believes that her brother, Adam, lives in a special home and is greatly loved there. She still mentions him on occasion but now that we have a new baby, she dwells on him. We still tell her that Adam is different than her, that he needs special care which we couldn't give him, that he's OK and loved and that someday we'll go and visit him. Someday we'll have to tell her about adoption and his new family, but she now thinks "special home" means that doctors and nurses are with him.

Lauren and Michael

My friend has adopted two girls. She explained to Bethany, age 4, that every baby has a birth mommy and a real mommy and that most times it's the same mommy, like for her and her brother, Joel, but Rachel has two different mommies.

Bethany had been very attached to Rachel and was very angry at us and would wake up at night crying. She finally told us, with much coaxing, that she was afraid that we were going to give her away. She said, "Yes, giving away—not nice." It was like an arrow through the heart. She's at peace, now, and having an open adoption has really helped. She knows she can see Rachel and still always be her sister.

Beth and Daniel

Our psychologist said he didn't think it was necessary to tell our son. I can't believe he said that. We plan to tell our son because this is something that happened to all of us, our whole family. He's too young to understand, now, but I think he should know someday, but when he understands the good and bad and pains of what life does offer.

Warren

I have always been concerned about how having two handicapped siblings would affect Nathan as he got older. He cares about his brother and sister a great deal, but I do think that the experience has left him with a lowered self-image and self-esteem. He learned early on that life is not perfect. Kids occasionally tease his younger brother who continues to be overweight, visually impaired, and equipped with twelve toes. I have never actually witnessed anyone teasing Nathan about his "defective" siblings, but I'm sure they have. Although they are not even three years apart in age, Nathan and Damon seem light-years apart in their abilities and interests. They are not the playmates we imagined they would be when we conceived Damon.

Barbara

My other daughter was only 18 months old when her sister was born. She knows nothing. She senses her Mom and Dad are upset and crazy but she does not know why. We will sit down with her when we feel she is mature enough to fully understand and explain it all. I don't want her coming back to me when she is married and asking, "Why didn't you tell me?" She will read all I am writing and I will explain why we made the decision and hope she will understand.

Eileen

Our older son was 3½. We told him his brother had a problem with his brain that the doctors couldn't fix and that he was going to live with people who could give him better care. He was 5 before he asked if the other people had adopted his brother. At the time he knew what adoption meant. We operated on the theory that if he asked a question, he should be told the truth, but if he didn't ask, we didn't volunteer.

He didn't seem overly concerned for the first year, but after that began to talk about it a lot, ask questions, and cry a lot. We took him to a child psychologist who felt that the baby with Down syndrome was not our son's only concern, but that he had learned that he would always get our attention by asking about the Down syndrome child. . . . He always seemed to be bring up the matter at inappropriate times (e.g., bedtime, chore time). Once we realized this we told him, matter-of-factly, that it was a sad thing to have happened, but we made the best possible decision and we were happy with our decision. If he wanted to talk about it more, he should ask again at a more appropriate time. He usually didn't.

As time goes on, he asks about his brother less frequently. He sometimes asks if he will ever see him. We usually tell him that we don't know for sure what will happen in the future, but that right now it's still too painful for us and that it wouldn't be fair to his new family. We also stress that the child with Down syndrome couldn't possibly understand who we are.

Hank and Mary Ann

We told our daughter that Jake was born with special needs and that Mommy and Daddy didn't think we could take care of him as we'd like to, so he's going to live with another family. She was tearful and said that she didn't want him to go; I cried and told her how sad I was about it, too, and reassured her that he was going to be with a wonderful family. . . . After about eight months, she stopped asking about him. I want her to know about Jake, but I'm not sure when or how to mention it. I fear if I do it too early, she may fear being abandoned, or announce it to people wherever or whenever, or simply not understand. Yet, I don't want to wait until she's a teenager and shock her. I do know that I will always tell her the truth.

Randy

Only recently, my 6-year-old has been asking questions about Nicole's delays. I have told her that Nicole needs extra help to learn things that just come naturally to her. I told her that Nicole goes to a special school and will probably always have to go to a special school. She didn't like that at all. She said, "Nicole better not need extra help by the time she is my age."

We haven't told her about the adoption. I am very concerned about how she will take the news. I am hoping that there will be counseling offered to her also.

Sue

It took a long time for our son to understand Nina's condition. He is now 12 years old. I have explained to Vincent that his sister needs special care and that I cannot be there all the time to take care of her. Nina's younger sister, Krystina, is 6 years old and does not comprehend the situation too well yet.

Pam

I have two cousins who were eagerly awaiting the birth of Emily. I explained to Jill, age 8, that Emily was like a girl she knows with Down syndrome and we couldn't take care of her, but we loved her and want her to have the best family possible, where she could be happy and have sisters and everything she needs, so we gave her to "the Smiths" who have another baby like Emily and wanted Emily very much to be her baby.

Michael, age 2½, repeatedly asked, for weeks, "Where's ooo baby?" until I finally described "my baby's day" to him in happy, simple terms saying, "Now Emily is waking up, her mommy comes in and picks her up and kisses her and says, 'I love you honey' and gives her a bottle. Then they go outside and play with her sisters, and she's so happy." I also told him that no matter what happened, if he was a good boy, if he misbehaved, et cetera, his parents would always be his parents. The confused look left his face, he laughed, and, to my relief, stopped asking, "Where's ooo baby?"

Jan

Our son is now only 2. He has been told nothing. He knew I was going to have a baby but he can't understand what's happened since the birth. He will be told when he's older and can fully understand what went on. It would be wrong to keep this from him. Since it's a genetic defect that causes spina bifida, he will have a need to know.

Ann

Hannah was only 1 when the baby was born. I think she has no memory of this now three years later. Joseph was 4 when the baby was born. We told him that the baby had something wrong inside. It was a problem that we couldn't take care of properly. There was another family that wanted her because they could take care of her better. He was concerned that she should have toys so he offered some to go with her. He also asked, one evening during bedtime book reading, "What color is the baby's throat?" thinking that if the baby is different on the inside, then its throat must be a different color. We said the baby was going to have a problem with her bones, that they weren't going to grow right. There were many times with my son that I felt like crying. The day Naomi left we all cried uncontrollably.

Max

We consulted a child psychiatrist. His advice was invaluable. We always told Joseph the truth, always answered the questions, and never ignored him. We offered explanations he could understand. We told him his mom and dad were very smart and could take care of him, but Naomi was different and needed a different mommy and daddy to take care of her. We assured him he was not going anywhere.

Rona

I told my kids that night [after the amniocentesis results] that our baby was a girl and that she had Down syndrome, that she could have a lot of problems, have mental retardation, she would look different, she'd need a lot of extra time and help, that when she's 30 she'd be like a 12-year-old. We talked for hours and cried a lot. We told them she could be very sick and she could die at a young age. They asked a lot of questions that we didn't have answers to.

A few weeks later, I had been talking on the phone when Amanda came in the house and I overheard Lisa tell her, "Mom's going to give the baby up for adoption." Lisa must have overheard my conversation. Amanda screamed and ran out the door. . . . I got them both back in and we sat on the floor and I tried to explain how I felt it was the best for Angela. I told them I was giving the baby life and that I wanted her to have the best possible life. . . . I told them it would be an open adoption and we'd know how she was doing and get pictures. . . . They tried to understand. . . .

When I told the girls that Angela was staying with us, they were so happy and excited they jumped up and down. Amanda pulled a letter out of her school bag written to Angela and telling her who she was and how much she loved her. Later, Lisa (age 7) wrote, by herself, "There are some babies who are born with

Down syndrome, no mattr [sic] what a baby has you should still love them. I love my baby sister and she has Down syndrome."

Cathie

My sister's kids were very excited to have a cousin. I told them the baby was too sick to come home; other people who are doctors and nurses have to care for her. I'm not quite sure how I will discuss it with my children when I finally feel they are old enough to understand.

Lexie

MARRIAGE

> Sometimes I wanted to be held and Jeff would hold me for a few minutes, then I would feel him tense up and pull back from me. He had "had enough." I think he recoiled at the point that his own emotions started to flood him.
>
> Jan

A crisis situation can put a tremendous strain on a marriage. Even marriages that were strong before the baby's birth may find the foundation shaking. There is a possibility that spouses blame one another for the disability and/or for the consideration of an adoption plan. Much of the time there is a great deal of anger associated with the grieving process and the spouse is the likeliest target for this anger that has no specific outlet.

Many of the couples who considered adoption found themselves very close during the process. Many shared similar feelings and reached the decision together without blaming one another. When couples were asked where they got their best support, many responded, "From each other." Couples who adjusted the best respected their differences in decision making and were understanding of the altering stages of grief. Barbara thought her husband wanted to raise April all along, but he supported her while she considered options. She said, "He listened to me, he discussed the options available with me, and he tolerated my ambivalence and mind changing. He promised to stand by me, no matter what."

Some parents do not share a closeness and have periods of blame and anger. Often one person will lean more heavily toward adoption than the other. The most severe problems occur when one parent wants to choose an adoption plan and the other does not. If a marriage is to survive this turmoil, counseling is almost imperative. It is often the spouse who feels most unable to cope who seeks help. If the other spouse refuses joint counseling, that is a message in itself to the person who feels helpless. Refusing counseling can create a great deal of conflict in the marriage.

Even couples who are in close agreement often need a counselor to help them resolve their feelings. No two people go through a grieving process in exactly the same steps at exactly the same time. One spouse may feel angry when the other feels at peace. One may still be in "shock" and denying when the other is trying to face reality. It is difficult to give each other support when thoughts and feelings may be conflicting.

Most couples who have lived through the adoption decision agree that the mother faces more emotional issues. She forms an attachment to the baby before birth. There is also a great societal stigma imposed on the "mother" who chooses an adoption plan for her child. Her grieving process may be longer and more intense. Many parents also have noted that men generally seem to be more withdrawn and less likely to discuss the loss openly. Most couples have received counseling for at least a few visits, some for much longer periods of time. The benefits of the counseling vary from couple to couple and are highly dependent upon the counselor's ability to work with people experiencing a great loss. Hints for choosing an appropriate counselor were offered in Chapter 3.

Parents Talk

We saw a psychologist, separately. He seemed to help us, but I think it would have been helpful to see someone else. . . . We were in agreement to give our baby up for adoption and felt relieved that we didn't have this huge burden hanging over our heads which, we felt, could have caused a strain on our marriage.

Lorraine

Our best support came from each other. We were, and are, in agreement on our decision.

Hank and Mary Ann

At first we were not in agreement. Dave felt that Jake was ours and we had to somehow make it work and that giving him up was abandoning him. . . . He knew I was leaning toward adoption, but I wavered in the midst of my total confusion. With counseling, Dave realized that he wouldn't be abandoning Jake, and I worked through all the guilt and feelings of failure as a mother. Then we began to work on "us" and through a forced choice exercise it became clear that our marriage was the most important concern to us.

We were always honest with one another about our thoughts and feelings concerning Jake . . . we never tried convincing one another. . . . When we became afraid that we were making the decision by indecision, we agreed to make a decision one way or the other.

Randy

Although we had both always felt that abortion was ethically and morally wrong, Donn said that he would not stand in my way if I chose to get an abortion. I was surprised to hear him say that, but I know he was thinking of me and how difficult it might be on me to have two handicapped children. . . . He was very supportive throughout the decision-making process.

Barbara

We had counseling with a psychotherapist from our church, who counseled us for free and saw us through the adoption. We also talked with a counselor from the Regional Center and with a former pastor. We've been through a lot but our friendship over the last nine years and our love and faith have been the key factors in our mutual healing, which continues to progress. We've both had a lot of anger at God and at each other, but we have a wonderfully honest and loving relationship which has only improved in depth through this crisis.

Beth and Daniel

We decided right from the beginning that our decision had to be made together and fortunately we are similar people and wanted the same thing for Adam. I really believe that had I wanted to keep Adam, Michael would have agreed to, but his heart may not have been in it. I probably was the real decision maker, since the mother is the primary caretaker.

We received counseling together during the three weeks Adam was home to help us sort out our thoughts and feelings about Adam. Michael stopped therapy after the adoption and I continued.

Lauren

Lee and I have been so supportive of each other. We feel that we have become closer, for we are all that we have now. We love and respect each other very much. We are our family and we cherish each moment together.

Julie

We went a few times [for counseling] but found the psychologist a little strange. She had told us to go home and tell our 18-month-old baby what had happened. I still get depressed over the whole situation, which isn't good for us, but I hope to get stronger.

Kathleen

That first moment we heard the baby's diagnosis, I imagined moving to a ranch-style house because the doctor said walking would be a major accomplishment for a child with cri du chat. That first moment for my husband was quite different. He didn't think adoption, but he surely knew this child wasn't going to be a part of his daily life. I was very hurt and angry by this. I felt he was insensitive and that I was the only "parent." This resentment lasted for a while, and our counseling sessions helped immensely.

Lexie

My husband still says after six years that he would like his son home, but deep down he knows it was best. . . . His love for me has gotten us through this. He wouldn't go for counseling, but I received it through family services. Our marriage has gotten stronger. We have survived the death of my mother, my father's remarriage, and five moves in less than six years. After Matthew, I feel that our marriage can survive anything.

Trudy

Our marriage is definitely stronger from what we've gone through and we're both proud of each other for doing a good job in raising our "special baby."

Mary and Rick

Our marriage has been strained because we have a disabled child to deal with daily. If anything, I think perhaps there is less stress on us since we have made this decision [to find an adoptive family for Nicole]. Only once [have we had marital difficulties since the decision was made] when Rick was having a bad day with Nicole, he made reference to the fact that he wouldn't have to deal with it much longer. I thought that was a cruel and inappropriate thing to say.

Sue

We made our decision together. Fortunately, my wife and I agree often, especially on fundamentals of living and of relationships. Rona was in therapy for a major depression; I attended some of the sessions. The therapy helped the depression and helped me to be a better husband for my wife, but the decision was all ours. I think we got closer.

Max

Max is wonderful. I feel so close to him after going through this together. Our marriage is even stronger.

Rona

Deep down in my heart, I knew Richard did not want to see Nina placed in a family care home. I think he blamed me for that decision. He never expressed his true feelings at that time. I never really knew how he felt. . . . After a while I tried to talk to him to try to get him to open up. It was very difficult—he isn't the type of person to let anyone in. He became very introverted and very moody. It was especially hard on me because I needed him and he wasn't there. I didn't know what to do.

After some time passed I think he knew how difficult it would have been to have Nina home with us. . . . Our marriage somehow has survived this terrible misfortune, but I cannot tell you how. It was hell.

Pam

We were supportive of one another throughout the decision-making process, but found that the whole ordeal brought up issues from several years ago. Our marriage had been shaky and had just settled into a semblance of stability shortly before Brian was born. We continued to receive counseling for about a year. We both feel confident that we made the best decision possible for our family, but there's a lot of underlying anger, which is not directly related to Brian, but to events and circumstances which happened before his birth.

Joanne and Bob

We weren't in agreement and can't really resolve this. There was no room for any give on either side so one of us had to [give in]. At first I was always blaming Kevin for not being strong enough to even try to see if he could handle taking care of our son. Things do get better, but for obvious reasons they will never be the same, because in the back of my mind I will probably always feel this way even though the biggest part of me loves Kevin.

Ann

Ann wanted to bring Michael home. I talked her out of it. She told me that I denied her the chance with Michael and maybe I did. My concerns were for Michael's best interests, Gregory's best interests, and my marriage to Ann. If we brought Mike home I don't think any of these would have been met.

Kevin

There were times in the first few months when I wanted to talk and cry about Emily, and Jeff was unable to be there for me. I think it had to do with our different styles of coping with pain and loss. Jeff could only cope with his sadness for brief periods. He distracted himself with TV and activity. . . . Sometimes we would argue. I was angry because I felt he should deal more directly with his emotions and I wanted him to be able to comfort me for as long as I needed it. On another level I realized that he had a right to cope in his own way, as I had a right to cope in my way. Eventually I learned to get support from other sources when Jeff couldn't provide it.

As a whole we did very well. We learned that we could count on each other . . . that we treasured and valued each other . . . that we could bear to lose almost anything, even our baby, if we could still be together. Our marriage was very strong and stable before Emily, and it was undoubtedly strengthened even more as we lived, worked, our way through the loss of our baby.

Jan

Frank and I aren't married, but he is Angela's father and has been by my side through everything. At first, Frank was very adamant that I should have an abortion and we had several big fights. I stood my ground and refused to be pressured into something I didn't feel I had the power or the right to decide to do.

Later, we agreed totally that adoption was the best thing for Angela. We made the arrangements for the adoption and found a perfect family. He was set, his decision was made. . . .

After a month of struggling with my emotions I made my decision to keep Angela. I told Frank. To say we had an argument would be putting it mildly. It was more like an atomic bomb went off! As he left my house that night I was told I'd see him in court. . . . It wasn't overnight, but he did finally see that I was capable of raising her. Now, he's happy I took another stand and went against what he thought was best and went with what I felt in my heart.

Cathie

We felt like we were on a roller coaster. When we first found out our daughter had Down syndrome . . . Louis would lie in bed with the pillow over his face. I sat in the living room crying to my mother. . . . We were on different wavelengths and not communicating at all. . . . Finally, I went in to him. . . . We poured our hearts out to each other. I told him how inadequate I felt. He told me how he sees women on drugs, pregnant, and some who throw their baby in the garbage. . . . Why couldn't we get what we hoped for? He felt guilty about giving the baby up for adoption. It felt like a car; if you get a lemon you return it. . . .

We went for counseling. I sat on one side of the room, he on the other. . . . The therapist advised us to go gently on each other, not to be so hard.

It seems like there is an awful lot of stress in our life and marriage right now. The smallest thing will set me off. I tend to dwell more on it. He feels he is being strong by not talking about it. . . . He says I'm a very strong lady. I don't feel like that, but we do draw strength from each other. . . . We stand by one another and together we are taking small steps to recovery.

Eileen

Note to New Parents

Family issues often can be a painful part of the decision-making process. It is helpful to remember that members of your extended family are feeling a loss, too. Your parents will grieve the loss of their expected grandchild. In addition, they probably will feel sad for you and the pain you are experiencing.

Your questions about your other children can best be answered by experienced professionals, especially your pediatrician or family doctor because he or she will know the children. Openly admitting to your children that you may not be the "perfect" parent can be painful. Yet, children are quite resilient, and with love, patience, and honesty, most are very accepting.

Your marriage is probably a major concern. Be patient with one another, respect each other's feelings, and keep the lines of communication open. Compromises may be necessary. Refusal to share and openly discuss your feelings can only lead to problems later on. Keep in mind that adversity often strengthens a marriage and most couples often say they've become closer no matter which decision they made.

Legacy of an Adopted Child

Once there were two women
Who never knew each other
One you do not remember
The other you call mother.

Two different lives
Shaped to make yours one.
One became your guiding star
The other became your sun.

The first gave you life
And the second taught you to live it.
The first gave you a need for love
And the second was there to give it.

One gave you a nationality
The other gave you a name.
One gave you the seed of talent
The other gave you aim.

One gave you emotions
The other calmed your fears.
One saw your first sweet smile
The other dried your tears.

One gave you up.
It was all that she could do.
The other prayed for a child
And God led her straight to you.

And now you ask me through your tears
The age-old question through the years
Heredity or environment—which are you the product of?
Neither, my darling, neither
Just two different kinds of love.

Author Unknown

6

Adoptive Families

> The geneticist told us he believed there was a waiting list of people seeking to adopt children with Down syndrome. That was a shock to our systems—to hear of a waiting list!
>
> Randy and Dave

One of the questions new parents frequently ask is, "Who would want to adopt a baby with a disability?" Many parents question, "If I don't want my own child, who would?" When they find out that there is a waiting list for children with disabilities, they wonder, "Then what's wrong with us? Why can *they* do this if we feel that we can't?"

All people are individuals with different strengths and weaknesses, with different values and expectations. One new father, whose newborn had several medical complications in addition to Down syndrome, was very concerned about the "kind of people" who would want to adopt his baby. Bob F. talked with parents who had adopted a baby with Down syndrome before choosing an adoption plan for his son. He described the qualities of these parents for the new father by saying, "Some men choose to become priests and give up ever having a wife and children. That doesn't mean that choice is best for everybody. People who choose to raise children with special needs aren't 'better than us,' they're just different."

Parents who choose an adoption plan for a baby with a disability have various reasons for doing so. Likewise, parents who choose to adopt do so for a variety of reasons. There is no stereotypical couple who chooses to adopt a child with special needs. Some of them are very religious people who feel a "calling." Most are nurturing people who do not fear the possible lifetime dependency. Some have had close contact with a person or people with disabilities. They may have had a family member or a friend with a disability. They may have worked with people or children with disabilities. Some may have a birthchild with a disability and they know that they are capable of parenting such a child. The family who adopted Max and Rona's baby had adopted two girls with dwarfism. They were looking for a third girl with a similar condition to complete their family. Many families may already have a child with a disability and may, as the family who adopted Max and Rona's baby, want another one in the family to help their other child or children feel less different.

Most adoptive parents don't see themselves as "special" people. They feel that raising a child or children with disabilities is something that they *want* to do and can do. They admit that they have chosen it, whereas parents who give birth to the child often feel as if they have had the choice made for them.

Adoptive parents usually have an extensive preparation process to help them determine if they are capable of parenting children with special needs. Special needs adoption agencies often run classes with thought-provoking exercises that help couples decide what kinds of special needs they would be willing to accept or feel able to handle. Unlike birthparents, adoptive parents can pick and choose the special needs with which they feel most comfortable. Many parents who give birth to a baby with a disability wish that they could have been granted the same choice.

In some states, adoptive families receive monthly stipends for caring for children with special needs. Birthparents in these states may worry that these people may be adopting only for the money. Parents who are concerned that money is a motive for adopting a child need to explore the situation carefully before choosing an adoption plan. The majority of families who adopt have worthy intentions and the money is used as needed for daily expenses to care for the child.

FAMILY PROFILES

The following families have offered to share their feelings on adoption and how adopting a child, or in some cases more than one child, with disabilities has affected them.

Lynn and Bill

> A child is a child and a special gift. I feel we'd accept any child, regardless of their handicap. After all, we all have handicaps in one

way or another. Everyone needs love and deserves a chance at a
"normal life."

Lynn

Lynn and Bill have five children. Billy, 16, was adopted as an infant.
Lori, 14, Becka, 12, and Ryan, 10, are their biological children. Meghan,
7, who has Down syndrome, was adopted when she was 12 days old.
Bill is a vice-president of a construction firm and Lynn is a homemaker.

Meghan was premature and spent the first six weeks of her life in the
intensive care nursery. Her birthparents decided soon after birth that
they were going to make an adoption plan. Lynn and Bill were contacted
by the adoption agency because they had adopted Billy through the
same agency. They had no previous experience with Down syndrome.
They spent some time educating themselves about Down syndrome and
discussed Meghan with all of their other children. The family agreed that
they had plenty of love to give and that Meghan needed a loving family,
so they adopted her because "we all needed each other."

Lynn and Bill feel that the only "special" quality they have for parenting Meghan is "lots of love." Lynn says:

She is treated like our other children. Her brothers and sisters still fight over who
gets her and she's the first one they go to when they get home. She's included in
all their activities and with their other friends. The older children have learned a
lot from Meghan. She's the topic of their essays and they always get an "A" when
they write about her.

Meghan's winning battle with leukemia has strengthened the family
spiritually. They all feel they are stronger and more understanding of
others' problems and are "better" for having her in their lives. Lynn admits that it's difficult to describe the depth of her love for Meghan. She's
convinced that Meghan's arrival into their family was "meant to be."
When asked if they have any regrets Lynn vehemently responds, "No
regrets at all—ever! We'd love another little girl just like her, but there's
only one of this very special little girl!"

Lynn and Bill offer:
To Meghan's birthparents:

Your decision has made a big, wonderful difference in our lives. You have
given our lives something special. Over the years the love doesn't wear off—it
grows, just like it does for all our children. She is our sunshine every day. We will
love this child beyond words forever.

We are no better than you because we feel we can love this child; we all have
our special place in life. Please know that we think of you often and always on
holidays and birthdays. Our child (yours and ours) will always know that she
was given up out of love by you.

Thank you for our child and may God bless you.

And to new parents:

We appreciate the decision you are trying to make. You are wonderful people to be able to recognize that you can't give your child what he or she needs. There is nothing wrong with you for knowing you can't handle it. It's too bad that you have to go through so much pain to give others such joy. There are many people waiting and praying to love your child. You are good people for the decision you are about to make.

Ben and Eileen

> A normal life at our house is Mike and Anya being there and being themselves.
>
> Eileen

Ben and Eileen are the parents of four children. Anna, 15, and Matthew, 14, are their biological children. Michael, 14, has Down syndrome and was adopted at the age of 9 after living with the family as a foster child for about a year. Anya, 10, who also has Down syndrome, lived with the family for three years as a foster child before she was legally adopted at age 7.

Eileen had an older brother who had Down syndrome but died before she was born. Her mother was told to place him in an institution at birth and to "forget you ever had him." Although he was brought home occasionally, he lived in the institution until he died at age 5. She also had an uncle with cerebral palsy who lived with her family for fifteen years.

Eileen and Ben ran a Community Training Home shortly before considering adopting their children with special needs. Their interest in becoming foster/adoptive parents was sparked by watching an episode of the television show "Quincy," about a child with Down syndrome in a foster home. Both Eileen and Ben still work in a sheltered workshop, he as an instructor and she as an instructor/aide. When they applied for a license to be foster/respite parents, their home study was so extensive that Eileen says, "They even wanted to know what kind of toilet paper we used! (Only kidding, but very close to the truth.)"

Eileen and Ben feel that all children need a loving, caring home life to help attain their maximum potential. They both have a genuine love for children and feel their sixteen-year marriage is blessed with love and consideration for one another. They describe their home life as "normal for us. Crazy, but normal." Anna and Matthew have been great advocates for persons with disabilities and have made great teachers of their peers. Eileen has found her nursing background helpful, and both Ben and Eileen have proven to be strong advocates for special education.

There is no contact with the birth families of their adopted children.

They are agreeable to, and would welcome, communication with some of the biological family members, but previous abuse of one of their children would cause them to prohibit any association with certain family members.

When asked if they ever have regrets, Eileen responds:

I think regrets is the wrong word to use here. We have had moments that we felt we were crazy for adding this on to ourselves, but thank the Lord they were few and far between. Sometimes we wonder what we would be doing now without them and we wonder if our biological children, Anna and Matthew, would be the unselfish, caring teenagers they are today.

Ben and Eileen admit that they feel inadequate to understand the feelings of birthparents, having not had that birth experience. They do offer the following advice:

Children with disabilities can live within the family unit. Use all the social services and advocacy groups available to you.

Giving up a child for adoption is a lifelong decision. It may be harder to live with that decision than learning to love and nurture your child at home.

Martha-Jean and Robert

Each child gives something special to the family unit. Our expectations run both high and normal. I guess we see it as each has their own pace in life (sort of the different drummer thing) and our role is to guide them along a path of success. What we see is a flower opening when its time is due, not on some developmental chart.

Martha-Jean

Martha-Jean and Robert are the parents of eight children. Their family consists of two birthchildren, Jason, 14, and Daniyel, 13. Their other children have been adopted; one they have coguardianship of. Noah came to live with them at age 2 and is now 9. He has multiple disabilities. Jennifer came to live with them at the age of 3, is now 8, and is emotionally delayed. Hannah was adopted when she was 2 weeks old. She was premature at birth and drug-addicted. She is now 6. Faith, 6, is a foster child who has multiple disabilities. Adam, 4½, has Down syndrome. Joshua is 2 and has Down syndrome. Another adopted child, Ryan, died at home at the age of 2. Ryan was anencephalic (very little, practically no, brain) and they knew he would have a short life span. Martha-Jean felt "very blessed with the time the Lord gave us with him."

Martha-Jean describes the home studies they have had as "very intense, at times it seemed almost intrusive." They were asked to write personal biographies and were interviewed separately and together and also with their children. Questions ranged from personal likes and dislikes to what their childhood, adolescence, and young adulthood were like. They had to describe their relationships with their parents, with their siblings, with each other, and with others. Questions were asked about discipline, parenting, religion, dysfunctional families, education, and children with disabilities. There were four or five interviews with the social worker before the home study was complete. With each new adoption, an update is done which requires two visits, each two hours long.

Martha-Jean and Robert will not adopt a child older than their oldest son because they don't believe in "unseating his eldest role." They prefer to adopt infants under the age of 2. They adopted two children with multiple disabilities before considering children with Down syndrome. They were on a waiting list for about six years after applying to a number of agencies. After the first contact with the National Down Syndrome Adoption Exchange, they found Adam and he was in their home within two weeks.

Both parents worked with children with Down syndrome in an institutional setting and always enjoyed their personalities. They were impressed with the survival skills and development within a very restrictive environment. Martha-Jean grew up with a girlfriend who had Down syndrome and had a very close relationship.

Martha-Jean says it's very hard to explain why they have chosen to adopt these children:

It may sound a bit corny, but we really feel our gifts are from God. . . . Our mission is being parents to our children; our talents have been there through our whole lives. It's something that just comes naturally to us. We have always been elated when we brought our children home. It has always been a real family affair with relatives and friends involved.

When asked their opinion of the birthparents Martha-Jean says:

I think the decisions are very different and individual. I have no right to judge and they actually end up giving more to their child than if they kept them. I think it would be nice to have contact. We don't feel threatened as parents and we understand and respect other people's choices. Sometimes we feel sorry that they are missing out on knowing what their child looks like or is like. I would like to see some shared parenting happening for children who have special challenges in life.

And of regrets:

On a really bad day I wonder why I am a parent at all!!! But I have no regrets. Sometimes I wish we had started at a younger age so we could have more . . .

but the reality is that it is lifelong parenting. After school there comes supportive employment, supervised living (hopefully an independent apartment), and there is always the crusade to help the general public to accept our children, young or grown, for the individual people they are.

Martha-Jean and Robert offer the following message for birthparents:

No one will ever walk in your shoes. Go with what is right for you. Just be sure your decision is made after you have received accurate information.

Think about sharing the life of your child even if it is only once a year. It will help with your questions of what and who your child looks like. We think many adoptive parents would be open to this.

Stephanie

These children *are* my family life. Every priority, decision, activity, and project must be considered with Teddy and Rachel Joy in mind. Each day has to benefit each of us.

Stephanie

Stephanie is a single parent who has adopted five children. Three of these children have died. Misty was adopted at 9 months with severely involved cerebral palsy and heart and lung damage. She died at 5 years of age from secondary complications of pneumonia. Wendy was adopted at 16 months. Her diagnosis was Rubinstein Taybi Syndrome. She died of a ruptured cerebral aneurism at age 2½. Laura Kate had been left in the hospital to die because of her multiple medical complications (the doctors had recommended this to the birthparents). Stephanie heard of her and adopted her when she was 5 weeks old. She died about six months later following open-heart surgery.

Stephanie adopted Teddy at 25 months. He has Down syndrome, mild CP, a seizure disorder, and vision deficits. Rachel Joy (biological daughter of Beth and Dan) was adopted at 4 months, has Down syndrome, is deaf, and has severely limited vision.

Stephanie admits feeling very depressed upon learning of Rachel Joy's deafness and limited vision. She felt sad for her whole family, because communicating with Rachel Joy has become so complicated and she is not sure if Teddy will be able, or willing, to learn signing.

When asked her reason for choosing to adopt children with special needs, Stephanie states:

I refer to my lifestyle as one of ministry. Just as other Christians are called to be missionaries, teachers, doctors, nurses, et cetera, God has called me to raise these children. I am completed by having them in my life. I do not yearn for marriage, vocation, money, or other amenities in this life. When people comment that I have my hands full, I say, "No, I have my whole life full." I feel contentment in the fullest sense—blessed by God, enriched, and fulfilled.

I am constantly being told that I am special and wonderful and that others couldn't do what I do. I tell them, "Hogwash!" For what God calls us to do, He also provides the strength and resources. Most often, my support system is our church congregation. People get an opportunity to see that my children are cute, appealing, and valued. Once their hearts are caught up, the friendships and support come easily. What's really fun is when they start thinking, "Gee, maybe I/we could do this, too." People need to realize that all parenting has its stresses and issues; some of them are different issues when the children are handicapped, not necessarily harder, just not as common.

Stephanie does not have contact with the birthparents of Laura Kate or Teddy. The birthparents of Misty and Wendy "became extended family" and she maintained an open relationship with them while the children were alive. She has a friendly relationship with Rachel Joy's birthparents, Beth and Daniel.

Stephanie expresses joy at accomplishments each of her "little ones" has attained. For Teddy, "mobility has been a struggle, but, literally, step by step, he's stepping out on his own."

Stephanie was asked if she would consider adopting another child with special needs. She expressed no regrets about adopting her children and offered:

I'm not sure if God is through building my family yet. Each time one of my children dies, I just know I won't adopt again. But, God does the healing. The miracle work is complete and I become excited as each child arrives in my life.

Her family wasn't complete at the time of her interview. About a year later she adopted 16-month-old Jonathan who has Rubinstein Taybi syndrome.

Stephanie sends a message to birthparents that shows her acceptance and understanding of parents' struggles when deciding about an adoption plan for a child with a disability:

Dear hurting birthparents,

I know these must be sad days for you. A birth experience has ended, not with tears of joy, but with tears of sorrow. It's probably hard for you to believe that someone else has been hoping and praying for a child with [a disability]. You may even feel guilty that you are not able to raise this child yourself.

But, oh, birth family, God has equipped each of us to do different things. Try to be grateful that you have recognized that this is not your job, and grateful that He has raised someone up who feels equipped.

Your value as a person is not diminished because of this choice, just as I don't think less of myself because I could not handle the stresses and issues of working in an office forty hours each week.

May God begin His healing work today in your lives. Thank you for the gift of this child.

Love,
Stephanie

Our Child

Our child
Can never be not yours,
Nor not ours.

So somehow,
We must let you know
Our unbound gratitude
For this precious gift you nurtured
Then gave into our keeping.

Thank you for sharing life,
For allowing it uterine maturity
In place of abortive non-existence
Which you could have chosen.

Thank you for
Caring deeply,
For trusting enough
To place your babe into a small secure ark,
To float into the rushes of life
Without even a Miriam at watch
To tell you where
His growing path will be.

We honor that trust,
And we shall love and cherish him
As strongly and surely as you do.

Our child
Will grow tall and well,
Undoubtedly with the stumblings
And skinned knees of life.
But always we will be there;
And you also,—in spirit, close by.

A mother's spirit knows no abandonment,
No matter what circumstances
Produce separation or distances.
Our child will always know that you care.

We pray for your joy and well-being.
We humbly acknowledge your gift,
And in spirit closeness
Share with you OUR CHILD.

Chris Probst
West Jordan, Utah

7

Finalizing an Adoption Plan

MORE DECISIONS

> We offered a very feeble, unbelieving prayer to God that if this was
> His will (which we doubted) and if it was all right with Him (which
> we doubted), would He please provide a loving, nurturing Christian
> family for Rachel where she would be treasured and cherished. The
> very next day Stephanie appeared at our door. She had heard about
> us through a mutual friend and was very anxious to talk to us about
> adopting Rachel.
>
> Beth and Daniel

Before deciding upon an adoption plan, many parents need to investigate the procedures for adoption and consider the types of adoption
available. Other parents may feel that it is fruitless to spend time examining the procedures for and the possible openness of adoption until a firm
decision is made. Again, this is an individual choice. Often the mother
and father may disagree about the sequence of these steps. Each person
must deal with decision making in his or her own way and each parent
should try to respect the needs of the other. If one parent feels the need
to learn about the way the adoption may be arranged even before firmly
choosing adoption, then the other should respect these wishes. It may
be comforting at the end of the struggle to know that everything was
thoroughly investigated and that an informed decision was made.

CLOSED OR OPEN ADOPTION?

> We don't visit our child and I know we never will. We don't want
> our wounds opened up again. There is a thin layer over the wound

now and we just can't risk having that ripped off again exposing the
raw, painful wound.

Eileen

Many parents, when offered the adoption option, immediately think
of the single, pregnant, teenage girl who relinquishes all rights to her
child never to see or hear from him or her again. Even this situation has
changed somewhat in recent years and adoptions have become more
open than in the past. Many parents are not aware of how open an adoption can be.

Special needs adoptions are somewhat more flexible than are adoptions of "normal" infants. The degree of openness can vary. Some birth
families and adoptive families visit each other in their homes. Dan and
Beth have a very open arrangement with Stephanie. They visited often
soon after the adoption, but less frequently as the months progressed.
Beth says: "I was Rachel's mommy for three months and somewhat attached, although I never got that 'mommy feeling' I so much prayed for.
I needed the transition period and so did my other children, especially
Bethany. We visited every other month for six months. We talk less now
but still keep in touch."

Some birthparents choose to have no contact with the adoptive family
either before or after the adoption plan is finalized. Mary Ann and Hank
chose a closed adoption even though the adoptive parents would allow
contact if they wished. "We could get word about him through another
family who know the adoptive family and see them periodically. It's too
painful for us to do so."

Most families reach an agreement somewhere in between. Joanne and
Bob have visited with the adoptive family twice in the two years since
Brian left their home to join his new family. They talk by phone about
once every two months and request pictures. Some parents choose to
meet the adoptive parents initially either in person or by telephone, and
then to continue contact by telephone or mail, often requesting pictures
about once a year. Lauren speaks often with the adoptive mom: "She's
wonderful and I wish I had a piece of her in me. I know about all of
Adam's doings and accomplishments. This is the only way I could let go
and give up this baby—if I could watch over his life."

Other parents choose to have an intermediary, usually the adoption
agency, relay news of the child. Lorraine shares her feeling about third-
party contact: "It means a great deal to me to know that at any given time
I can make a call to see how our baby is doing. I never pester anyone but I
feel comfortable knowing and hearing that our baby is doing well." The
situations vary from family to family. The degree of openness usually is
agreed upon by the families, sometimes arranged by a third person.

Some adoptive parents would like to have at least some degree of contact with the birthparents who do not wish to hear any news of their birthchild. Others may feel threatened by the birthparents' desire for contact and may not agree to it. The fear they have of losing a child for whom they have been waiting may seem unwarranted to the birthparents, but is very real for some people. Jan and Jeff have a closed adoption. Jan shares:

We didn't exactly choose this. I would have preferred the possibility of some type of contact; however, if we wanted to let Emily be adopted by the foster family who took her from the hospital we had to abide by their wishes. We could have saved lots of money, fourteen months of expensive child support, and had an open adoption if we took her from that family and went privately. We wanted what was best for Emily so we trusted that this family really loves her and is committed to her.

Adoptive parents sometimes will agree upon an open adoption and then have second thoughts after they have the baby, perhaps expecting that the birthparents will get on with their lives and no longer desire to see the child. Birthparents should be cautioned that though an adoption is "written" as "open," control over provision of pictures, letters, and visitation rests in the hands of the adoptive family. Agreements generally are based upon trust rather than legalities since adoptive parents retain all legal rights to the child.

Parents must carefully examine their feelings about the openness before choosing an adoptive family. A careful match may avoid problems in the future. Randy and Dave arranged an open adoption although they didn't and still don't want contact: "We thought if at any time in the future we change our minds that the option will be available." Initial agreement about the maximum amount of contact the two families will have allows adjustment for less contact in the future. Usually the desire for frequent contact diminishes as both families go on with their lives.

Parents Talk

We have a guardianship agreement which will probably end up being an adoption. I don't think that I will ever see her because it will hurt too much and probably will not accomplish anything. . . . If I want to do anything for Laura, they will let me. I feel comfortable with them, believe in them, and trust them, which makes me feel good and I can sleep at night knowing she is safe and in a good environment.

Kathleen

I have requested a letter and picture of the baby from the adoptive parents. I think this will hurt in some way but make me feel good in another way. We do not choose to see the baby because I think this would hurt us too much and open up some of those wounds that are starting to heal.

Lorraine

I would like to hear that Maria is doing just fine. But, a picture—I'm not sure if that will help me or hurt me.

Warren

Dan wanted it closed because of warnings from various people about potential conflicts and residual pain, but we chose an open adoption. Before visiting I felt a little nervous. During the visit I was glad to see her. After the visit I felt firm about my decision. . . . I now truly feel that Rachel is Stephanie's daughter. I have my two kids. I see myself as a surrogate mother. I just wish that I could have given Stephanie a child that was in better shape, but she is happy with Rachel, and the disabilities don't diminish who Rachel is to her like it did for Dan and me.

Beth

At first, we used to visit, but realized in the long run for the sake of both families, the personal contact should stop. We stay in contact by phone, letters, and sending pictures. We are comfortable with the situation as it is now. . . . At this point, I actually feel that Matthew is their child and not mine.

Trudy

Our adoption is closed. Quite frankly that was all that was offered to us other than institutionalization which I wouldn't allow. We signed her over to the state and lost any contact at that moment.

Lexie

I could never have given him up not knowing the family or his whereabouts. We plan a first visit next month. I had to wait until I had another baby or else it would have been too painful. I anticipate the visit to be very sad for us. I only hope that I like his family and home to reinforce that it's for the best.

Lauren

I wish adoptions were more open. At first I didn't think I would like to have any contact with Michael's new parents, but now I wish there was more that could be done to see him.

Kevin

I had to know where Jake was going to live and to have talked with the adoptive parents. I felt that I had to have some control over what actually happens to my baby. I would never disrupt his family because he's theirs now, but knowing I could contact the family if I wanted to brings me much comfort and peace. I can't imagine requesting photos; I think that would really sadden me, as would details of his life.

Randy

We have an open adoption. We could never have done it any other way. We get letters—they are still hard to read. They are a very sweet couple and inform us on Hollie's progress. But now it seems it is too often, so we are reevaluating the time for contact. It just seems to bring us back and it's so hard to hear about her.

Julie and Lee

We disagreed, at first, on whether to have an open adoption. Bob wanted it closed; I wanted it open. We finally agreed on an open adoption. As time goes on, it feels more and more as if he is their child. Each time I talk with the adoptive mom, I'm reassured about my decision. Their love for him is so evident, and she openly admits the trials of parenting, which reinforces our belief that this second child, especially one with a disability, would have placed a tremendous strain on our family and on our marriage.

Joanne

We do have an open adoption, but we didn't meet the new parents and don't want to. What if there was something about them I didn't like? Trivial little things that would haunt me? I have an image in my mind of them and that's OK. I didn't want to know their address or phone number because I may get obsessed and start calling every day. I have to give them some room. After all, she is not my baby anymore.

Eileen

We are looking into open adoption. I would like to keep a certain amount of contact with Nicole—how much, I don't know yet. The idea of her being gone is still rather abstract. I can't fathom how I will feel about visits once we actually relinquish her.

Sue

Before I decided to raise Angela myself, I had chosen an adoptive family, a super couple who had other special needs children. I spoke with them and the agreement was that I'd get pictures and be able to see her once a year.

Cathie

I don't know if I had an option, but I would have chosen closed anyway. She should be part of her new family and they should take care of her and I don't have a right to interfere because this would cause prolonged confusion and pain for her and for me. . . . If she is having skeletal problems I don't want to know about it. What could I do about it? They will do what they think is best.

Rona

The agency has a letter from us which can be accessed by her when she is 18 if she wants. I must say that while we are the biological parents which results in a certain organic bond, the cultural parents are the ones who take on the seemingly simple but most difficult task of raising a child to be a well-adjusted adult and it is with them that the strongest bond should form. Having it closed was policy and also recommended by everybody.

*Information was relayed via the adoption agency social worker. . . . The news
was good and we were relieved and we could get on with recovery.*

Max

*We see Nina once or twice a year. [Nina lives in a family care home, a guardi-
anship agreement.] I try to call the family care mother to see how she is doing or
she will call me. Again the guilt surfaces because I feel she can take care of her
and I can't. It is still very difficult for me to see Nina. I have in a way cut myself
off from her. She is 10 years old now. It bothers me to see her just lie there and
not know anything. After seeing Nina I get depressed and wonder how it would
have been if she was even a little different, more responsive, anything.*

Pam

CHOOSING AN ADOPTIVE FAMILY

> We gave a basic profile of the type of family we had hoped to find
> for Jake. Most importantly, we wanted to be convinced that they
> would love him just for who he is.
>
> Randy and Dave

It is possible for parents to have some control over choosing a home for
their child. A counselor from an adoption agency or exchange may be of
help in this respect. Some parents are very selective about the type of
family they want to adopt their child. Others feel that any parents who
are willing and able to accept their child will be suitable. Adoption counselors usually suggest that birthparents develop a list of criteria to help
them sort out circumstances and characteristics they feel are important
for their child's future family to have.

Points for birthparents to consider when choosing an adoptive family:

1. Do you want your child to be placed with a single parent or a couple?
2. Do you have a religious preference?
3. Is the age of the parents important?
4. Do you have a preference over the locality—near your home, within your
   state? Would you prefer that the child be raised in the country? a small town?
   a city?
5. Do you want your child to have older brothers and sisters? A large family or a
   small family?
6. Does the financial status of the family concern you?
7. Is the educational background of the parents important?
8. Would you consider parents who have had no experience with children with
   disabilities?

9. Do you want a family who will agree to have contact with you?
10. Do you want to meet the family in person? By telephone? (This could be arranged without giving identifying information.)

Some parents develop a list of criteria and come to the realization that they are looking for a family just like their own. It is at this point that these parents may decide that adoption is not the choice for them and they choose to parent their child. After considering adoption, Barbara and Donn decided to raise their baby themselves. Barbara said:

I started fantasizing about who would be the best parents for our daughter. Since LMBBS is such a rare syndrome and so few people, including people in the medical profession, know much about it, I thought that the best people to care for our little girl would be someone who was already familiar with the syndrome. Then, like a bolt of lightning, it occurred to me that *we* would be the best people to care for this little girl. . . . We already had one child with the syndrome and were familiar with its characteristics and challenges. And we had always wanted a little girl.

Parents who continue the search for an adoptive family usually adjust their criteria as they review information about available families. One of a few potential families usually is chosen as the "perfect" family for which they have been searching. Birthparents who reject family after family are probably not ready to make an adoption plan. They need more time to sort through their feelings and possibly may need to reconsider their decision. Professionals who work with birthparents should be prepared to offer, or arrange for, intensive counseling for these parents who seem too "picky."

Parents Talk

We saw a videotape of the family and met with them four times. We had to meet them, to know them, to trust and believe that they would love her and care for her forever.

Julie and Lee

We chose the family out of three choices given to us. We spoke to each other a dozen times before we surrendered Adam.

Lauren

Friends who we knew from the center that provided early infant stimulation adopted Matthew. We chose this because that family knew Matthew from the age of 3 weeks, when we met. We knew they wanted him very much, had so much love for him, had a big family and no financial worries. We knew Matthew would be well taken care of.

Trudy

The agency will present the family. Rick and I will approve of them.

Sue

The baby lives with twenty other disabled children. A woman and her husband and family dedicate their lives to these children. There are five other children with Down syndrome, so Laura will never be alone without a brother or sister who is like her. I made this decision [guardianship] so that I would know what type of environment she will live in and for my mother so she can talk to Laura's new mother. The family is not rich, but will give Laura the emotional support which I could not give.

Kathleen

We chose the family, but only spoke by telephone. We choose to not have any other contact.

Hank and Mary Ann

We contacted the adoption coordinator from the Little People of America who forwarded to us profiles of five families who wished to adopt a child with achondroplasia. We were not to know identities or exact locations, but we did know family makeup, educational status. . . . We picked one family. That family was approved by their local authorities. We sent along a letter to the adoptive parents and we received several months later a Christmas greeting card with a picture of the baby and her two sisters who also are adopted and have achondroplasia.

Max

We didn't get to choose the family, but we did get to meet them. We explained why we were going the adoption route and they understood. These people now have six special needs children in their family.

Kevin

We didn't meet the family, but wanted to know everything about them. They sounded like the perfect parents for our daughter. A nurse at the hospital who got close to us when we were going back and forth to see our baby told us that when she met the adoptive parents she was so impressed by how wonderful they were. Her exact words were, "Lorraine, if anyone could be better parents for Maria than you and Warren, it would be these people." Our lawyer said the same thing after he met them to turn the baby over to them. This felt very reassuring to us, hearing from people we knew and trusted.

Lorraine

About three weeks after we had decided to search for a family for our son, our social worker had found four families to choose from who did not meet the criteria that we had listed. I left a meeting with her and said to my husband, "If that's the best they can do he's coming home." (He was in foster care.) Two days later, we got a call that she had found another family, their home study had just been completed, and they, miraculously, met every criterion on our list.

Joanne

I spoke with the new mom on the phone because I wanted to make sure the baby got there safe and sound. It was so awkward. I was afraid she would not love my baby enough and she was afraid of losing the baby. We danced around each other not really saying much of anything.

Eileen

We didn't choose or meet the family, but we did approve completely of the choice. If we had not, we wouldn't have allowed the initial placement; we would have had her placed privately.

Jan and Jeff

We were really excited when we found out Stephanie had been praying for a female infant with Down syndrome whom she wanted to name Rachel! We also found out that she began to have a strong desire to adopt another baby the third week of July, the same time we found out the girls had Down syndrome. Even though we knew that adoption was the right thing for us, it left us with feelings of desolation, fears of being socially ostracized, and lots of guilt. But after meeting Stephanie we both felt a joy and peace and excitement that never went away. Our only fear was that Stephanie was too good to be true!

Beth and Daniel

LEGALITIES

> We felt very angry and powerless. We were infantilized and would never use a public agency again. We paid $420 a month for fourteen months. We are still, sixteen months later, trying to get our insurance companies to pay the last of her extremely expensive medical bills.
>
> Jeff and Jan

In spite of the fact that open adoptions are not legal in many states, many parents have reached agreements either by choosing a private adoption or through a special needs adoption agency. Agreements often can be reached that work for all people involved. The laws on adoption vary from state to state. Parents should be very cautious of the legal "red tape" that can occur, especially in arranging an adoption across state lines. Adoptions within a state are much more quickly arranged. A family lawyer may be necessary to protect the interests of the birthparents. Sometimes, a local adoption agency can represent the birthparents satisfactorily.

Various hindrances can occur with the adoption process. Sue and Rick learned that because Sue is an American Indian their adoption proceeding was subject to the Indian Child Welfare Act (ICWA) which gives the tribe jurisdiction over where and with whom the child may live. Every tribe is different. It is important to learn at the beginning what procedures the particular tribe follows. Another family was denied the right to relinquish by an assistant district attorney who determined that the family was "emotionally and financially capable" of parenting their child. Through effort and persistence an adoption was finally arranged, yet the frustration of making a decision and then being denied was emotionally devastating.

The fees for a special needs adoption are usually not exceptionally high. Some adoption agencies operate with funding that absorbs costs. Birthparents may need to hire a lawyer to represent them and sometimes if the child is moved to a home far from his or her place of birth, the birthparents may be expected to pay travel expenses for the baby or for the adoptive parents.

Different states have different laws governing the adoption process. In some states there is a "waiting" period of a few days after the birthparents have signed the papers during which they may change their minds and take the child back. Birthparents may be asked to sign a waiver to this right. In some states the adoption becomes final for the birthparents as soon as the papers are signed or shortly after, but the finalization for the adoptive parents does not occur for several months. The child is a ward of the state or the agency, but will be living with the adoptive parents, under supervision by the state or agency.

Many states and agencies require that medical histories be obtained from the birthparents as a part of the adoption records; a few currently require genetic records. A report from the Social Issues Committee of the American Society of Human Genetics in *The American Journal of Human Genetics,* May 1991, recommended that all state and private agencies be encouraged to collect genetic histories. The American Academy of Pediatricians also was lobbying to make these reports mandatory. Parents who choose adoption for their child should expect to be asked for this information, a vital addition to his or her record, especially if the adoption is closed.

Parents Talk

A Christian adoption service did our adoption at no charge to us or to Stephanie. They felt it a special case and don't usually do special needs adoptions. We wanted Rachel raised in a Christian home and the state would not have assured that, but this agency would if Stephanie didn't work out. We relinquished Rachel to this agency which placed Rachel in a foster care situation until the adoption could become final. Stephanie ran into some "red tape" because the agency was new at special needs adoptions and didn't know how to do all the stuff she needed for funding, et cetera.

Beth and Daniel

We did a private adoption through Janet Marchese. We had spoken with Catholic Charities but did not like the fact that Maria would have to be placed in a foster home. The private adoption allowed us to find out all about the adoptive parents and to have some contact, too. Our lawyer was also kind, helpful, and very supportive of our decision. The lawyer fees were $500.

Lorraine and Warren

I chose a guardianship which was arranged by a lawyer. The only fees I had to pay were to the lawyer who handled the paperwork.

Kathleen

We used a county agency and social workers for the adoption. There were no fees involved. The baby had to become a ward of the county first to assure the adoptive family of financial aid for the child. The red tape took a long time to untangle so the baby was not formally adopted until he was 18 months old, but was living with his adoptive family during this time.

Mary Ann and Hank

We worked first with the hospital social worker then the adoption agency social worker. We consulted a lawyer, but we didn't need her. Fees were waived because of the infant's abnormality.

Max

Social workers and the state Department of Children and Youth Services handled the adoption. There were no fees involved and the adoption was arranged privately, approved by the state agency. Matthew was technically in foster care, but with his adoptive family until his final adoption papers came through.

Trudy

The lawyer hasn't sent a bill, yet. He asked if any money was exchanged between families, and we said "no." His cousin had gone through the same thing. He was very compassionate and put us at ease.

Eileen and Louis

Adoptions in our state are generally closed. That didn't set well with us, so we arranged a private adoption, using the services of the National Down Syndrome Adoption Exchange, a social worker, and a lawyer who has worked with other special needs adoptions.

We ran into some problems because we were originally told that the county where Jake was going to live would take care of the adoption papers, and then . . . we were told it couldn't be done that way because the judge feared that if the adoptive parents were to change their minds, the county would be responsible for a handicapped child. Then we were told that our own county could do the paperwork, but only if we agreed that the county could place Jake where and when they wanted and we'd have no say and never learn of the outcome. Finally, we found the lawyer who handled it smoothly and quickly.

Randy and Dave

Our lawyer was an acquaintance who must have really felt terrible for us because he did our adoption at no charge. We paid the adoptive father's travel expenses.

Lauren and Michael

Our social worker from Catholic Charities spent a great deal of time calling around the state and to other states. She found the family through a special needs adoption agency and they took care of the paperwork. When we went to court, we relinquished the care of our child to this agency with the verbal agreement that if the adoptive family did not work out we would be contacted to choose another. The state law allowed six days to change our minds; we signed a waiver to this agreement. The judge seemed more concerned about a paper we had to sign which allows the court to open records when the child turns 18. . . . Brian went home with his new family that day; the adoption became final about six months later. There were no fees for us.

Joanne and Bob

The wheels of Department of Social Services move slowly. Emily wasn't adopted until she was 14 months old. During the waiting time I felt in limbo. When people asked if we had any children, I drew a blank in my mind—did we have a baby, or not?

Jan

FINALITY—SIGNING THE PAPERS

> I felt like a part of me curled up inside and died—and like I failed my son.
>
> Ann

Parents who have chosen an adoption plan for their child often become very nervous at the prospect of appearing before a judge or a lawyer to sign the papers that give someone else the legal rights to their child. It is difficult for most parents, but many relate a less painful experience than they anticipated. For some, the final signing is a relief; once the decision has been made, it is easier to go on with life. Others may experience a second grieving process.

Parents Talk

I was nervous. . . . The judge was sympathetic, understanding, and did not waste time with the procedure.

Warren

I felt very sad, but a sense of relief at the same time. We had plenty of time to think over our decision, so we felt we knew what we were doing. We chose to have our lawyer hand the baby over to the adoptive couple; it would have killed us to be there.

Lorraine

We felt sad, relieved, scared that we might be making the wrong choice. It was an empty feeling, like having experienced the death of two children, the healthy child who wasn't born to us, and the "replacement child." . . . It would have been too painful to have been present when the adoptive parents took the baby.

Hank and Mary Ann

It was the worst day of our lives, other than the day when we found out about her brain damage. . . . I was in a daze. It was cold and drizzling that day. It was raining in my heart—my heart was gone.

Julie

We felt relieved, happy, grateful to God and Stephanie. For Rachel, I felt it was a second chance at a happy birth experience. We signed the relinquishment papers at Stephanie's house. When we arrived there was a big sign on the garage door, "It's a Girl! Thank you, Lord!" Stephanie was ecstatic to "give birth" to Rachel.

Beth

I was frightened when a sheriff came to our door with the papers. The finality was also frightening, but I knew it was right. I went to the hospital with the adoptive mother to pick up Matthew for his release. We drove to her house and then I went home alone. I felt good. Matthew had a great home and I could finally get on with my life. My decision was made; I was not in limbo any more.

Trudy

I was in shock. I was devoid of feelings at that particular minute. I had to do this.

Rona

It felt very unreal. Heart-rending. But there was also resolve and the culmination of a month of painful deliberation into this definitive and final act from which there was no return.

Max

I was present when the baby was placed with her new family. I felt relieved and sad, but I knew I had made the best decision for the baby and for the rest of us.

Kathleen

I was heavily drugged with tranquilizers. I was very nervous, despite the medication, and I was in disbelief. It was an ugly situation. I felt awful. I will remember that most of all. I remember and experience this day every year because that was the day she died in our hearts.

Lexie

We had ten days from the time we surrendered Adam to change our minds and get him back. I knew that I would never want him back, but I could let go and it wasn't final, yet, so it made it easier. The day he left was the saddest day of my life. I was so miserable and empty inside. I died inside and it's so vivid in my mind and always will be.

Lauren

My wife and I were both present [when the baby was handed to his adoptive parents]. It was a devastating day, picking up Adam's adoptive father at the airport, having to ride with him in silence from and back to the airport, thinking that this person is going to bring up our child. I had second thoughts about our decision, pain rehashing and thinking, "Why us? Why are we even being put in this position?" I wanted the day to end and to try to learn to go on with our lives as best as possible.

Michael

I felt like a bad mother with little self-worth. It was the second saddest day of my life. We signed the papers on a Friday and the new parents signed the papers on Monday. The family that had Jake in respite took him to the courthouse to the new parents. We couldn't cope with going through another goodbye, so didn't inquire about seeing him at the time of the adoption.

Randy

I felt like I was copping out, like I was attending the funeral after a four-month wake. I had a lot of second thoughts, but knew the adoptive family was thrilled with the prospect of parenting Brian and were nervously awaiting the call that he would be theirs. . . . I wanted to be there to hand over the baby, but was advised by several professionals that it would be "too hard." We did meet with the adoptive parents and drove them to a clinic to pick up the baby. The mother hugged me and reassured me that everything would be all right. I still regret that I didn't go in with them to see their joy as they met their new son.

Joanne

Walking up to the lawyer's office my feet froze. I said to Louis, "How can we give up our baby?" I felt like the scum of the earth, a real lowlife. But we then remembered how much these people want her and how much more they will be able to give her. We had been through a lot and wouldn't be here if we didn't believe in our decision. We sat down on the steps, held each other and cried, took a deep breath and went in to sign our baby over to another couple. Hopefully, it was and is the hardest thing we'll ever have to do in our lives.

Eileen

I felt terribly sad and empty, uncaring about life's details and supported by Jan in my sadness.

Jeff

I signed the papers very soon after Emily was born. I was still in a daze, numb. The real trauma was going to court, declaring out loud, in family court, that I was making an uncoerced decision that was absolutely irrevocable. As soon as I finished repeating the necessary words after the judge, I ran out of the courtroom and sobbed in the bathroom for about thirty minutes.

Jan

Note to New Parents

Whatever you are feeling is OK. It is not unusual to feel frustrated with the "system." Rules and regulations can be particularly annoying and though meant to protect all parties involved can sometimes seem to be unnecessary obstacles.

If you're feeling ambivalent, that's quite "normal." Not many parents are 100 percent sure of the adoption decision. You may need to take time away from decision making. Distance from the intellectual decisions sometimes allows feelings to surface. Be assured that you will ultimately make a decision for you and your child that will be best for all of you.

If you have second thoughts shortly before signing the papers, take time to reevaluate your decision. Though some states do allow a period of time for birthparents to change their minds, it's better to sort through your feelings *before* you sign the papers. Consider the implications to yourself, your child, and the adoptive parents before you choose adoption with the intention of possibly changing your mind in the future.

When finalizing an adoption plan for your child, you should think carefully about the future. Once you've signed the papers, the decision is final.

The Road Not Taken

Two roads diverged in a yellow wood,
And sorry I could not travel both
And be one traveler, long I stood
And looked down one as far as I could
To where it bent in the undergrowth;

Then took the other, as just as fair,
And having perhaps the better claim,
Because it was grassy and wanted wear;
Though as for that the passing there
Had worn them really about the same,

And both that morning equally lay
In leaves no step had trodden black.
Oh, I kept the first for another day!
Yet knowing how way leads on to way,
I doubted if I should ever come back.

I shall be telling this with a sigh
Somewhere ages and ages hence;
Two roads diverged in a wood, and I—
I took the one less traveled by,
And that has made all the difference.

Robert Frost

8

Living with the Decision

EXPLAINING TO OTHER PEOPLE

> We needed to make sure people understood that what we did was the best thing, not the easy thing.
>
> Hank

Years ago when doctors recommended that parents place their children in an institution people seldom talked about the child. The family lived with their "secret" and the friends who knew about the child accepted that the family had merely followed their doctor's advice, an honorable "choice." Today doctors dictate to parents that children do best in a home environment. The societal expectation is for the child to be in his *birth* home environment. In addition to the pain of choosing a better life for the child, parents who choose adoption also must deal with the guilt imposed by societal condemnation. Some parents may find themselves "explaining" while others may choose to hide their "secret" with lies. One mother shared her perception of the societal attitude: "Our alternative care decision for our children has no cheering section. I think we all feel the real or imagined scrutiny of the general public but we must look beyond that. Many people do admire our strength and courage."

In spite of the stigmas, many of the families who contributed to this book were still open about their decision. Many felt a need to let people know what their final decision was. It may, in part, have been an explanation, but was also a way of having control over timing—if the parents volunteered the result of their decision making, others wouldn't be asking them about it. Several parents sent a letter to friends and family to inform them of their choice and/or to thank them for the support. Parents who had not yet returned to work also found this a helpful way of avoiding uncomfortable questions from colleagues.

The following letter was sent by Joanne and Bob to inform friends and family of their decision:

Dear . . . ,

You are one of the many people who has been supportive of us through this most difficult time in our lives. We'd first like to thank you—without the friendship and understanding you have given us, we would have been floundering for a much longer time. The decision we've made has not been easy. It is the most painful choice that we've ever had to make.

We have had hours of counseling by professionals. We have spent days, and many sleepless nights, soul-searching. We've spent hours and hours talking to parents of children with Down syndrome, to parents who considered adoption but have kept their children, to parents who have relinquished their children, and to adoptive parents. We have found these people to be helpful, understanding, and, for the most part, nonjudgmental.

As we talked to these people we looked for similarities between them and us. We looked at coping strategies, strengths and weaknesses, and the ability to accept. We learned a very valuable lesson—each situation is unique and is complicated by the differing personalities of the two parents. We finally realized that our decision could only be made based on our current life situations.

As we watched Brian develop into a little person with a lopsided smile and an engaging personality, we experienced a desire for him to have the best of care and learned also to closely examine our personalities and our strengths and weaknesses as parents. Brian could stay within our family and be subjected to the outcome of the huge amount of stress we've been experiencing over the last few months, or he could move on to a family who have been waiting for a child, who have the time and energy, dedication, love, and the thrill of having him come into their lives. Our lives are still tinged with the disappointment which in time would have faded, but coupled with so many other problems may not have dulled in time to give Brian those special first three years which are so crucial to his development.

We have carefully chosen a family and will remain in contact with them. The pain for us will never be eased by the joy of watching Brian develop or by the love that children with Down syndrome so typically give. We have chosen a different path and hope these gifts will come to be for his new family. We hope that we have become more understanding people. We hope that we will be less judgmental of others and we hope that the pain of these last few months will deaden with time.

We still firmly believe that Brian was meant to be, as so many of you heard us say throughout the pregnancy. Letting go took courage that we didn't know we had. We do love our son and hope that the life that we have chosen for him will grant him the ability to achieve to his fullest and that his parents will give him the opportunities that we felt incapable of.

You have touched Brian's life as we're sure that in some small way he has touched yours. You have given of yourself when we needed you. Thank you, from us and for Brian.

Sincerely,
Joanne and Bob

New parents may find it particularly difficult to face acquaintances. Simple statements are usually best. Following are some of the questions other parents had and responses they used that served to close the conversation:

Q: What did you have? A boy or a girl?
R: I had a boy, but there was a problem.

Q: Where's the baby?
R: —There was a problem and she's no longer with us.
—Things didn't work out as we expected.

Q: Don't you have two children?
R: I had two pregnancies; I only have one child.

Q: So, how's that new baby?
R: —Fine.
—We lost the baby.
—Something happened and we don't have our baby.

Q: Do you have any children?
R: Yes. Well, no. She was a special child and she is with a loving, special needs family.

If people persist in trying to get more information than parents care to talk about, the comments "It's really quite painful to talk about—I'd rather not" or "It's a long story and I'd rather not go into it here; maybe some other time" should be helpful.

Parents who feel a need to give more of an explanation to some people might offer something like: "She/he had (spina bifida, Down syndrome, microcephaly . . .) and she/he is living with another family." Comments like the previous ones usually open the conversation. Parents who openly told acquaintances, and sometimes even strangers, about their decision often found these other people sharing a painful story of their own.

Most parents found people in general to be nonjudgmental and supportive. A supportive response heard by many parents was, "That must have been a hard decision," which is, of course, an understatement, but it does show caring and an attempt at understanding. Other comments that have been supportive were: "You did the right thing; I would have done the same" or "You must really know yourselves well to be so honest." A friend of Trudy's, the father of a child with Down syndrome, told her, "No one knows what you are going through and no one has the right to judge unless they have walked in your shoes."

There are those few people who will be judgmental and who will express their judgment with cruel words. Lauren and Michael were mistaken for their in-laws and an acquaintance said to them, "How could they do such a thing—these children need more love than a normal child." Kathleen was told, "You were always so compassionate to people and animals, so why are you doing this?" A comment that often is voiced by well-meaning people, but which usually evokes feelings of guilt is, "Of all the people I know, you're the *best* ones to have a child like this." Another, very guilt-inducing remark heard by many couples was variations of "You never know what might happen to your other children." Although these remarks are not as common as the supportive, kind words most people give, they are very painful. Parents who choose adoption should be prepared for the possibility of hearing harsh comments.

It is difficult to find appropriate responses to judgmental questions and statements. To the people so intent on wondering how they could do such a thing, Lauren simply responded, "You don't know—you're not in our shoes." Randy and Dave responded quickly to someone who suggested that "God chooses special people to have these children," by agreeing, "Well, maybe so, and we're searching hard to find those people." Usually it is best to assume that people who say cruel things are simply insensitive. Often *no* response is the best response.

Parents Talk

It's difficult telling people our decision and facing the fact that we gave our baby away. I didn't want to go out of the house and face people. I guess in a way I am ashamed of myself that I couldn't live with my own child being this way. I still have a difficult time at work because at any given time I can run into someone who might ask about my baby not knowing what actually happened. I find this very difficult and draining.

Lorraine

I have only told a handful of friends and fellow workers what happened. Others knew of Maria's problem and would ask how she is doing. To this date nobody asks me how she is. They may ask sometime and I hope I have the strength to be honest.

Warren

One of the hardest things was going back to work. There were 200 people who wanted to say they were sorry and wanted to help but there was nothing they could do. I got upset a lot because everyone asked how things were going and I didn't really want to talk about it.

Kevin

When acquaintances asked, I wanted to die. For the past year I've avoided people who may ask. I would duck them if possible. If, unfortunately, I was confronted I would say, "I had a boy," or "Things didn't work out," depending on how well or little I knew the person. I stopped going into the story of my life.

Lauren

I found it difficult to be around people who knew of our decision, people who I wasn't sure if they knew what had happened, of running into people that I anticipated having to explain to. I felt self-conscious and paranoid. Going back to my teaching job caused me much anxiety, it wasn't as difficult as I had anticipated, but it is still difficult at times to feel totally comfortable and at ease.

Randy

I never brought it up unless questioned by acquaintances, whereupon I said the truth. What they thought of me after that was not my concern.

Trudy

If the question came up, "Do you have any children?" I used to just cry and even tell perfect strangers about it. Now I guess I'm getting better and I don't feel right saying "no," so I say that I do (did) have a precious baby, but that she has special needs and is now with a new family. It is still so hard.

Julie

One friend said, "You can't adopt your daughter to someone else. If you do, God will do something worse to you." We responded badly and were deeply hurt by this and others like it. Thankfully, that kind of response was about 3 percent, as opposed to 97 percent supportive. Unfortunately, that kind of "help" tends to bring your own self-doubt and guilt to the surface. . . . We are still tender and it's hard facing the condemnation of the "mighty few." We feel isolated now, but our friendships have much better quality and are more satisfying.

Beth and Daniel

For the most part, if people didn't know the whole story, we simply stated, "We lost the baby." Talking about it was not a pleasant experience and we tried not to get into it with people who didn't already know what was going on.

Mary Ann and Hank

Most acquaintances left us alone, for they were so embarrassed when I'd respond that we lost the baby. They felt they had opened a can of worms. You do learn to put up walls and protect yourself from any unnecessary pain.

Eileen

The hardest people for me to face have been the high school students that I teach. I was a teacher one day and the next day I was the parent of a baby with Down syndrome. Many students had been very involved in my pregnancy. I didn't return to my job until the following September, so the students were not as inquisitive as they might have been had I returned to the same classes. Most of them didn't know that there had been a problem, so I just answered their questions of "How's the baby?" with "Oh, he's fine." The unexpectedness of the questions was difficult. I'd be caught up in the day-to-day affairs of teaching and suddenly be reminded of the whole ordeal of the past months. It's still uncomfortable for me, but I know that with time it will get easier.

Joanne

To some people I just said, "I had a girl," and that was that. Some people I told I had a miscarriage and some I told about the horrifying mess.

Kathleen

After the initial shock almost everyone we talked to was very supportive. I must admit that I felt pressure to be sad and devastated around people even during those short amounts of time that I felt calmer and less depressed.

What I tell people varies from I don't have a child to telling them that I had a baby that I gave up for medical reasons. It is still very uncomfortable and makes me sad.

Jeff

I felt no obligation to give any answer other than what I felt like saying. We don't owe anyone an explanation.

Jan

I became deeply depressed. . . . I began going to different cleaners, grocery, hairdressers, et cetera, but when it was inevitable I said she was very sick.

Lexie

For a long time I would only say that I have two children because I did not want to explain. The guilt was always there. I could not bring myself to explain this situation to other people.

Pam

The baby looked fine. The average person didn't know there was a problem. After she was gone, I stopped going to the dry cleaners. He kept asking about the baby, trying to be nice and friendly, but I couldn't deal with it any more.

Rona

GRIEVING

Unless you're faced with this, no one can understand what it's like. To tell someone we grieved for the child we expected to have, they don't understand that to us a child died and we had to go through the grieving process for that child and then accept our special child and then decide what was best for that child, ourselves, and our existing families.

Cathie

Parents who have chosen an adoption plan for a child with a disability often express grieving two losses. They grieve the loss of the child they expected and didn't get and then grieve the loss of the child they gave birth to and "gave away." Eileen expressed it as three losses: "I lost my dream of a healthy baby, I lost her to adoption, and I lost her period. No baby. The baby I carried for nine months. It is almost like a death, only worse. Not many people can understand." Julie expressed her grief: "I grieved the loss of Hollie's quality of life—a kind of universal unfairness for her."

Parents who experience the loss of a child whether it be the expected one or the one that was born to them usually experience most of the stages of grief. Depending upon the length of time between the birth and the finalization of the adoption plan, the two grieving processes may be concurrent. There is no particular "order" to the grieving process and there is no "right" way to grieve. Most people tend to move back and forth, from stage to stage. They may feel angry—at life, at themselves, at their spouse, even at their other children. Joanne remembers, "Sometimes I'd look at Katie and as much as I loved her, I'd be angry because if she hadn't been so wonderful, perfect, and healthy I wouldn't have attempted another pregnancy." A few months after Rachel's adoption, Beth said:

Now that the "dust has settled," so to speak, I am finding I have a lot of anger inside. So is Daniel. We tend to take it out on each other. Even though we look the same on the outside, inside there's been a fundamental change. And some of the sugar-coated illusions of life have been stripped away and we are seeking to make sense of it.

Most parents feel an intense sadness which eases with time. About six months after she signed the papers, Eileen shared:

I used to cry every day. Now I seem to cry every couple of days, which is also getting less and less. Sometimes I feel as though my heart has cracked and I'm crying it out of me. It flows out with my tears. I have such a void in my life. It's an empty feeling. She will always have a special place in my heart and I shall never forget her.

Jan shares:

It's impossible to describe what it's like to have a baby inside your body for nine months and then to lose that baby. It's so bad that you have to spend a lot of time shielding yourself from the pain. Defenses go up. Many times now I can't clearly remember the whole truth of that emotion myself. I have to push it away so I can go on, as if life were still routine and normal.

The grieving process may take months or even years. The fact that the child is still alive and living with another family may make resolution, or peace, a little more difficult to sustain, whether the parents maintain contact or not. Parents who have lost a child to miscarriage, stillbirth, or death and have also chosen an adoption plan for a child express that they experience more resolution with the death than with the "letting go." With death, there is finality; with adoption, even if the choice is one's own, there is no "end." A few months after the adoption, Beth expressed her grief: "I cry for my lost children, but I know I wouldn't want it any other way because of their Down syndrome. And so I even feel robbed, in a way, of my grief. If your child dies, you can walk away honorably in the eyes of others—but mostly in the eyes of yourself."

The research that has been done on birthparents who have chosen adoption has dealt primarily with unwed, young mothers, but it substantiates many of the feelings that older, married men and women face in the aftermath of a finalized adoption plan for a child with a disability. One study determined that the birthmother's ability to adjust was greatest if her own wishes were followed. Those who were not allowed to develop and follow their own coping styles had more difficulty in later years. The best adjustments were made by those who received support and had opportunities to talk about the event. (Seijo, Lois, "Effects on Birthmothers," *The Roundtable, Journal of the National Resource Center for Special Needs Adoption,* 3.1 (1988): 3.) Couples who chose adoption plans for babies with special needs will attest to the fact that they felt "better" for having been given the opportunity to choose what they wished for their child. As stated previously, each person and couple must deal with each situation in the way that makes them feel best about their decision.

INNER FEELINGS

Most of the time, I am happy. I'm an optimistic kind of person. But, you know, there's that underlying sense of tragedy. That sense of being connected with the world's pain that I never had before. And even though 95 percent of those I know have been supportive, there's a sense of isolation.

Beth

Most of the literature written by parents raising a child with a disability indicates that these people often feel isolated. For parents who choose an adoption plan, there is a double sense of isolation. They no longer feel the same as friends who have never experienced any childbearing loss, and they often feel isolated from those who have suffered the pain of giving birth to a child with a disability because of the choice they've made. Many couples feel rejected by parents from the parent support groups because of their choice. Whether the rejection is internal, external, or both, the feelings are very real and very powerful.

Many parents, particularly mothers, express feelings of inadequacy in parenting their other children: "If I 'gave away' my baby, what kind of mother am I?" These insecurities with parenting have lasted for a few weeks for some parents, for others a few months, and for others longer than a year. Feelings of little confidence in parenting do lessen with time and confidence does get stronger. In the state of grieving people often isolate themselves from others and don't share the child-rearing stories with friends as they did in the past. Sharing with other parents will help birthparents identify which behaviors their other children are exhibiting are "normal," and alert them to behaviors that may need attention by a professional.

Perhaps the hardest test for most parents who choose adoption is accepting their own limitations. It is very difficult to admit to oneself, as well as to others, that someone else might be able to love your child more unconditionally than you. Most of the parents who have willingly chosen an adoption plan are mature, loving, conscientious people, who have examined themselves and bravely faced their personal limitations.

Nicole is still at home with her birth family. Sue and Rick are looking for an adoptive family. Sue remarks: "I have had people tell me, 'You are so strong; I couldn't handle it.' I just nod and say, 'Thank you,' when I really want to scream out, 'I *can't* handle it!' " Beth expressed her feelings: "I still have sadness and guilt. Not sadness for Rachel—I know she is in the best hands possible. But sadness and guilt for my inability or unwillingness or whatever you would call it, to raise my daughter." At the time of her son's second birthday, Joanne wrote, "I feel mostly sad about myself and my limitations—that I can't be one of those mothers who 'does it all.' "

Parents who choose adoption often find it difficult facing other people because parents have their own thoughts as to what others may be thinking. Most parents experience what they refer to as "paranoia." It is common to feel that "they" all talk about "us" and "what we did," or of wearing the "scarlet letter"—"Yes, I'm the one who gave away my baby." These feelings diminish with time. A few years after the adoption, one mother said, "I have begun to believe in myself and my decision in a positive way. I don't feel as hypersensitive to what I 'think' other people are thinking or feeling. No one else is me."

Many parents continue for months feeling very vulnerable, very exposed—"Now I *know* that bad things can happen to me." They tend to

worry when their other children get sick that it could be some fatal illness—"Is God going to punish me?" They may feel defenseless against
accidents realizing there's no immunity against tragedy. Hank and Mary
Ann felt very vulnerable when their next child was hospitalized with
bacterial meningitis at the age of 3½ months: "We had the empty feeling
that somehow, we were going to have to have a retarded child. (She's
OK, though.)"

Many parents overreact to situations that they may not have before. If a
spouse is late coming home from work there *must* have been an accident.
Emotions are fragile; they may cry more easily. For a time, they also may
worry less about minor annoyances in life. Randy stated, "Who cares if
my daughter spilled chocolate ice cream all over her dress, or the part in
her hair isn't straight?" With time and healing there is a return to a "normal" life, close to the old life, but not absolved from memories.

BITTER THOUGHTS

> My sister-in-law had a normal baby girl today. My cousin had a girl
> two days ago—ten weeks premature, but she's OK. I don't want to
> visit these babies. I want to steal them.
>
>   Jan

Many parents have expressed envy or resentment when watching
other happy families, in particular those who may have judged them,
either openly or subtly, for their choice. At times some parents think
vengeful thoughts towards other families ("If *you* had this happen to
you . . .") and immediately feel guilt because no one would wish this
pain on anyone else. Julie shares, "It's still so hard to see babies running
and jumping, doing all the things that will be so difficult for Hollie.
Sometimes I find myself resenting those mothers. They don't know how
lucky they are." Many parents have learned that families who appear to
be happy may have their own grief hidden within. To an outsider "we"
may now appear to be a happy, "perfect" family, yet there may still be a
degree of sadness.

Most women have bitter, angry thoughts when observing pregnant
women who seem to be so happy, so self-confident. Joanne remembers
"watching glowing, pregnant women and wanting to shout out, 'Look at
my baby! You could have one like this, too.' " Jan found it difficult dealing with pregnant friends, relatives, and co-workers: "I'm happy for
those I love who are pregnant, but I'm also envious and sad. I can only
take being with them for a certain amount of time." Thoughts like Joanne's and feelings like Jan's are common and although they cause guilty
feelings, these are normal reactions. One woman said, "It's not that I
really *want* something bad to happen to anyone else. I'd just like for

people who seem so judgmental of me, so happy and sure of what they would do if it were them, to be able to feel the depth of pain I felt so they could understand what it was like for me."

In spite of these angry thoughts, most parents become more in tune to feelings others may have when they experience a loss. Many parents expressed that they feel they have become more empathetic. Most try harder to be there for others, to send a card or note, to lend a listening ear. Eileen expressed her desire to help others, even strangers:

I heard of a woman who committed suicide when her baby with Down syndrome was a few months old. It was frightening to think that it could have been me and even more frightening to realize that there was so little control. I had no way of reaching that woman to help her. I felt like a failure, like I'd lost a friend.

PAINFUL ANNIVERSARIES

Mother's day is a day I seem to be particularly hard on myself. I wonder why I can't be like those "other" mothers who never lose their temper, never raise their voices, always have time to do anything their child needs done, always are smiling and full of energy, et cetera. I feel like a failure as a mother for one of my children even though I know our decision was the best one for all of us.

Mary Ann

The grieving process usually spans a time period of about one year for the majority of people. A significant loss, such as the loss of a child, may take longer. One-year "anniversaries" tend to be very painful for people who are grieving a loss. What may seem to be insignificant dates or holidays may bring unexpected reactions from those who are grieving. Sometimes the emotional reaction may take place a few days or weeks before the actual "date." People who find themselves depressed without being able to pinpoint the reason may be surprised. Jan has lived through two Mother's Days since Emily's birth: "The entire week leading up to Mother's Day is horrible. I am depressed, distracted, and irritable. It is the worst the day before, better on the actual day." The reaction may sometimes be physical—a sick stomach, tiredness. It may be vivid thoughts and memories, flashbacks in time, a general uneasiness, or the irritability and depression that Jan feels.

Holidays are particularly difficult for most parents. The "big" holidays such as Christmas, Hanukkah, Easter, Passover, Mother's Day, and Father's Day are usually painful, as are any holidays people find important within their families. Holidays that are usually less significant, such as the Fourth of July or Labor Day, could dredge up painful feelings, especially if the birth, signing the papers, or another event surrounding the decision-making process was near that day. Those who chose adoption have feelings of loss, the empty place at the table, the memories of "last year" when the pregnancy meant hopes and dreams of a future baby. Even parents who have chosen to parent their children may also express feelings of reliving the previous year.

The first birthday is usually very difficult because parents relive the pain and sorrow surrounding the birth. For parents who received the news through prenatal testing, the date the diagnosis was confirmed may be more painful than the birthday. Cathie answered the questions for this book a year after receiving the amnio results. She admitted that it was difficult to relive those early thoughts and feelings at the one-year anniversary of learning about Angela's Down syndrome.

Many parents recall the events of the previous year so vividly that it's almost like replaying a movie. Joanne woke up one morning a few days after her son's first birthday with the feeling that the baby was in the next room, with that all too familiar sick stomach, before she fully wakened. Jake's first birthday evoked a mixture of feelings for Randy, mostly sad and painful ones: "I remember bursting into tears on a few occasions as I vividly recalled his birth and of hearing the news."

There are several difficult dates that may vary from family to family or from individual to individual. The date the pregnancy was confirmed may be difficult for some parents. For many the one-year anniversary of the date they signed the papers triggers painful thoughts and depression. There may be a sense of unrest at about the time the adoption becomes final for the adoptive parents. Some parents may find their own birthdays depressing. A family tradition, such as returning to a favorite vacation spot, may cause some parents to feel sad. Joanne and Bob went camping the week after they signed the papers for Brian's adoption. A year later they returned to the same campground, even the same campsite. Joanne "thought it would be OK, but the memories were so vivid, the flashbacks intense. I was angry at my husband because he didn't feel any of it and seemed oblivious to the whole thing."

Usually the significant dates in the first year following the loss are the most difficult, and these days are easier to face in following years. Books on grief and loss may help parents become familiar with potentially difficult times to create an awareness of their feelings. There are usually helpful hints for working through these memories. (Consult the list in the appendix.)

Many parents experience pain when they see a person, especially a child, with a disability. Yet, most parents who have chosen adoption continue to search faces in crowds seeking out characteristics of the disability. It is not the searching for their own children as much as the curiosity as to what these children look like, how they act, wondering if the one they gave birth to looks like them.

Many parents feel pain at hearing newborn cries, at seeing other newborn babies, or other babies the same age as theirs would be. Jan shares, "Newborn babies make me sad. I just wish I could walk into a nursery or a maternity ward, pick one out, and take it home, especially when there are twins." Many parents compare development, wondering if their child would have reached those milestones yet.

Some mothers find it difficult to return to their obstetrician's office for their six-week checkup, and even on future visits, especially if they have not yet become pregnant with another child. One woman was sobbing by the time her doctor got to the examining room. The memories of being there, pregnant and happy, can be overpowering. Sitting among those happy, glowing, pregnant women and other women who have returned for their checkups with their baby in their arms can be especially depressing. Likewise, returning to the hospital where the baby was born can evoke vivid memories.

Most families have a difficult time when others ask, "How many children do you have?," "Is she an only child?," or "Do you have children?" With time, the responses get easier, but initially, there is the feeling of a child or one more child, but that he or she can't be mentioned or included. Joanne had to face several relatives and acquaintances at her mother's funeral before an adoption plan was made; the baby was in foster care. There were some very strange looks cast her way as she told one person that her daughter was an only child when others who knew that there was a baby, too, overheard her. Situations like this are painful at the time, yet, most parents look back later and find some wry humor in them. As parents become more comfortable with their own feelings there is less concern about what other people will think.

One of the most painful situations for most parents is when their other children ask about the disappearance of their brother or sister. In the decision-making process most parents are very concerned about their other children and the impact the loss of a sibling will have on them. (See Chapter 5.) Young children ask questions so unexpectedly that parents often are caught off guard and it brings the pain and memories back suddenly, in Randy's words, "like a knife through the heart." With time, the questions seem to let up and as parents reach their own acceptance, the answers become easier.

Parents Talk

Mother's Day and Father's Day were a little difficult for me but I know that Christmas will be harder because our baby was born shortly before Christmas.

Lorraine

At holidays, we will think, remember, and be sad.

Warren

The first year holidays and birthdays were so sad. We really felt a huge loss. The holidays were depressing but his first birthday was the worst. The whole last year was relived and I kept crying. This never should have happened. My second-to-worst time was my first Mother's Day after his birth. That was a real low day.

Lauren

Christmas was the first big holiday after the relinquishment. It had its sad, empty moments. I remembered the year before, fantasizing about the next Christmas with our new baby. I did contact Janet Marchese and asked her to call Jake's adoptive family for me. I had mixed feelings when Janet told me that "he is the center of their universe." I was happy because I wanted the very best for him, but sad because I wished I could have felt that way.

In spite of my sadness on Jake's birthday there was a part of me that felt the joy I knew his adoptive parents must be feeling so I sent them his birth photos and some photos we had taken of him. I knew that they would be thrilled with them and it gave me some kind of pleasure in sending them.

Randy

Christmas was still painful and sad, when our baby was 4 months old, but by Easter, we felt good again. We truly believe that time is the best healer, because with time, you see all the things your baby can do and you see that potential is there, that this baby will learn things, that he won't just lie in his crib totally docile. For his first birthday there will be a clown with ten friends to join all the fun and to have lunch, birthday cake, ice cream, face painting, and animal balloons. I'm going all out on this party, the same as I did for my other three children.

Mary

With Nicole in our family, I don't look forward to holidays, birthdays, and family gatherings the way I used to. I've lost a lot of the joy these occasions used to bring. [Sue and Rick were looking for a family to adopt Nicole when they were interviewed.]

Sue

Rachel's first birthday was last Friday, so writing this now has been difficult. A year ago we got the news and what often seems like someone else's life has recently seemed like it happened yesterday, especially hearing about Rachel's further disabilities. . . . We thought, "What would we have done if we'd decided to raise her and got this new news?" We were already devastated.

Beth

Holidays are extremely sad. I relive what might have been for her, for us. I feel these will always be awful days.

Lee

The first year was agonizing. We didn't think we had made a mistake, but we were still grieving and trying to conceive again. . . . It is so much easier for us to count our blessings now and to be happy for our child with Down syndrome and his adoptive family.

Hank and Mary Ann

I am not one to hold onto things or let feelings linger. I have a tendency to do what I have to do and adapt to changing circumstances. Although I did think of her on her first birthday (and I will think of her on every one of her birthdays), I wasn't crippled by thoughts and essentially I went about my day. My wife reacted much more intensely and had difficulty getting through her day.

Max

We did not request that Naomi be raised as a Jew. We wanted her raised with the religion of her family. In December, it's unsettling for me that my child is celebrating Christmas. I feel sad on every birthday, but feel happy for her that she is celebrating her birthday with her family. I wish my husband would cuddle me a little more on those days.

Rona

We haven't gone through the whole year yet—it's only been seven months. Christmas 1990 was really bad. Our son was born December 12 and that year was going to be filled with love and happiness, but it never turned out to be that way. We still had a celebration for our other son, but to us it was just another day. Every month on the 12th I remember he'll be one month older. I still cry, but mostly when no one is around to see me.

Ann

There haven't been any major holidays yet, and I'm not looking forward to Christmas or her first birthday. I do feel really sad every month on the 19th. It's another month. I think of her and how big she must be getting. I remember my first daughter and every little thing was a big deal. Sometimes I wish I could be a little fly on the baby's bedroom wall and watch her and observe, but not interfere. I know she's happy. I just hope I can be happy again.

Eileen

I was deeply depressed after the birth and surrender of Sara. At holidays I was bitter, angry, and sad, because I was supposed to have my daughter. The first two years I recounted every action of the birth, of the surrender, and recovery period as if it just happened.

Lexie

Looking back over that first year it was hard to believe a year had gone by. We had come a long way in that year and Angela had, too. We don't take holidays for granted, we're thankful she's with us, since we were so close to not having her here.

Angela's 16-month evaluation was not what I had expected. At 12 months she was doing so well, but since she isn't walking at 16 months, it brought her score way below what I expected. I felt as if I failed her. I realize I can't do that to either of us.

Cathie

In the beginning, family gatherings were very difficult. There was a deep feeling of emptiness. Nina's first birthday and Christmas were the worst experiences of my life. Till this day I get very depressed around Nina's birthday. I always wonder, what if the situation had been different and Nina was here?

Pam

I try to ignore holidays. I usually feel sadder and empty.

Jeff

Hardest for me that first year were the events which unexpectedly triggered feelings and emotions—I was more prepared for the "big" days like Christmas and Mother's Day. Something as simple as a bright spring day would remind me of the day my son was born. Even cleaning out the refrigerator sent me back in time to my pregnant self, moving into our new home with hopes and dreams of our future as a family of four.

Joanne

At holidays and her birthday, I am glad that April is a part of our family.

Barbara

At first, I was depressed at holidays, like something was missing, but life goes on and you have the choice to stay at a standstill and be miserable or go after what you want—happiness.

Trudy

Note to New Parents _____

No one can judge you if they haven't walked in your shoes. You don't need to explain to anyone, nor do you need to hide in shame. But you do need to protect yourself from hurtful situations as best you can.

You may be feeling less confident as a parent, as a person, even at your occupation. That's all part of the grieving process and quite normal. With time your confidence will return.

Part of the grieving process is the anger or bitterness you may feel towards those other "happy families." You are not a bad person for feeling this way or for having bad thoughts. Be easy on yourself; allow yourself time to heal. Don't try to fight the feelings, but let them flow. Each day will be easier than the day before.

It's time to renew our spirits,
And forgive what we may have
detested in ourselves,
And what we have hated,   .
For in the eyes of God, *all things*
are perfect,
Just as *He* has created.

Now it's time to renew our souls!
We have been through spiritual death.
We've walked, talked and felt as empty holes,
And have grappled for life and breath.

God never meant to hurt us as bad,
Or confuse us so much;
But chooses to use our physical beings.
We become conduits for His spiritual plans,
And cannot know His true reasoning.

However our destinies turned out,
Wherever our offspring lead out their lives;
Know that God has been guiding us,
Although reason can be well-disguised.

Now the past is past, and time to *reawake!*
We can heal while we hover from afar;
For it is not ours to judge ourselves,
But to carry on from where we are.

But if you don't know how I'll tell you,
Close your eyes and pray away that scar;
Know that in His plan for us,
All things are *perfect*, created as they are!!

J. B. M.

9

The Future

DOES THE PAIN EVER GO AWAY?

> It's been six years and I still feel as strongly as ever that I made the right decision. The pain never goes away, but does lessen with time. Sometimes I can't believe I survived that time period in my life, but I have and I am stronger for it.
>
> Trudy

Parents who chose adoption months or years ago can attest to the fact that, with time, the pain lessens and life does go on. Warren remembers:

At the time when Maria was ours, driving the hospital trips, the counseling and searching for the answers to all of this, I kept telling myself that my life will never be as it was before her. No one could convince me otherwise. But here it is one year and one child later and I am surviving through that sad chapter of my life.

Hank and Mary Ann relate, "It's been four years, and we still believe our decision is right for us and right for our child. . . . As time goes by we become more and more at peace with our decision." Parents who chose adoption express that they have changed either in some small ways or in several ways. All seem to agree that there is never a return to life as it was before the birth of the child with a disability but they begin a new life and move on.

At some point acceptance of the loss is attained, but most parents express a small amount of sadness that becomes a part of them. Almost all parents relate that they have grown from the experience, that they have changed in some way. Most don't proclaim to have become "so much better people" as many couples heard from the parents who are raising children with disabilities. Some of that feeling may be internal, yet much of it may be the external societal stigmas that are placed on people who choose adoption. However, life does go on and parents do regain happiness that they may not have felt possible.

Parents Talk

It's been two years and although at times I question if we could have coped, I know that we made the best decision [adoption] for all of us. I've finally begun to feel happy again and don't feel the bitterness and anger I used to feel. It takes a long time to recover and I know there will always be a bit of sadness within me, but healing does take place and life does return to a new normal.

Joanne

It has been four months since we went to court to sign the papers. I feel in our hearts we made the best decision for the baby and for Warren, Robert, and me. I could not imagine living the rest of my life raising a retarded child.

Lorraine

It has been three years, and it's still pretty intense when I think about it— which isn't that often anymore. Of course, one can find reminders everywhere, but now we know how to limit the impact.

Max

There's an ache deep inside that will never go away but I made the best decision for my family including Naomi. We'll all do better because of my decision.

Rona

It's been two months [since we decided to look for an adoptive family] and I feel that we are doing the right thing for both Nicole and our family. I feel a sense of relief that I won't have this cloud of depression surrounding me forever. I feel extremely guilty about this but it is the truth.

Sue

I feel it was the correct one [adoption] and though it still hurts, I don't regret it.

Jeff

It's been sixteen months. I know I did the right thing.

Jan

It's true what others say, "Time heals." I think of Jake every day, but not always in a sad, mournful manner. Sometimes, it's just a thought of "I wonder how he's doing" and at other times (in the extreme) I catch myself second-guessing myself. But I stay with those thoughts until I remember the process I did when coming to my decision and I have never regretted it. I do feel bitter at times that I had to be faced with such a decision and sometimes think, "Did this really happen to me?"

Randy

We signed the final papers six months ago. Even though I'm sad and torn, it was right for Michael.

Ann

I feel good about my decision [to have Michael adopted by another family]. I know it was right.

Kevin

It will be six years next January. I feel at peace with my decision, but I still feel very sad that the whole thing happened and that my husband and I were confronted with the most difficult decisions of our life at what should have been a joyous occasion. I used to think about Sara all the time, and now she doesn't occupy my thoughts daily. I always wonder about her, where she is, how she is, if she is alive. I fantasize that one day I will hire a private investigator to help fill my void.

Lexie

I realize with every day that passes that deciding to keep our son and raise him was the only and best decision for us. He is ours, just as much as our three other normal children, and having an extra chromosome or learning more slowly than our normal children was not justification to "place him." I tried it and just couldn't live with myself, or really like myself when I looked in the mirror. I couldn't try to pretend that I hadn't given birth to this special baby. Life was just not perfect and wasn't something I read about in a fairy tale. For the first time in my 33 years I was dealing with a major tragedy and in order to survive I had to gain strength from that tragedy and turn it into something constructive instead of destructive. I had a child's life at stake and I had to pull myself together.

I must add that these were reasons that stood out to me and I under no circumstance pass judgment on what other couples choose. It truly is and has to be each individual couple's decision. Every one is different and every marriage is different and there are different levels of strength held by us all.

Mary

It's been four months and my husband and I feel good about our decision [guardianship]. We just can't believe that it has happened to us. We just want to put it behind us and try to have a normal life.

Kathleen

It has been a year and two months since placement. Each day we try to come to peace in our way and feel more and more that she is in a good loving place and that perhaps someday we will know the answers more fully and that it will be clear and feel right.

Julie and Lee

It's been four months and I always hated the words, "Time heals all wounds," but it's true. I don't have that sick feeling in my stomach anymore. We feel comfortable with our decision but have good and bad days. If I see a child with Down syndrome, I stare and then I cry. I know I would cry every day if I had kept my baby.

Eileen

Life seems to have gotten back to normal after two years. We now have a normal, healthy, 1-year-old boy who has added much to our lives. We are all consumed with our daily activities and our family unit as it now stands without Adam.

When there is time to think back it is hard to believe the whole experience ever happened, but it did! There is still Adam living with another family, an experience that will be part of Lauren and me forever. Whenever we lose sight of our priorities we think back to Adam's birth and it puts the really important things in our life in perspective.

Michael

It's been almost two years since we found out Angela would have Down syndrome and a little over a year since my final decision [to raise her]. I made the right decision, there's no doubt about that. Even though I went through such pain and heartache I'm glad that things happened as they did.

It's scary if I look too far ahead. I don't know what is in store for us and I know it's not going to be easy, but I just feel I need to concentrate on this month, this day, and not worry about next year or ten years from now. I'll deal with that time when it gets here. I still worry that she would be better off elsewhere, especially financially, but I just couldn't give her up. It was killing me inside.

Cathie

It's been eight months and we feel better than ever. We're getting back to normal. . . . It has been the most tragic year of our lives, but it has also been a year of deep personal growth. We would have been happy not to have experienced such a devastating ordeal and such a wide array of emotions, but we also would have missed out on experiencing the grace and mercy of God and having a new level of compassion for others in similar circumstances.

Beth

It has been ten years since we placed Nina in family care. I still live with the guilt of not having her with us as a family. And I will always wonder if I could have had her home. I have great respect for the family care parents and am very comfortable knowing Nina is loved and cared for in their home. It has taken me a long time to adjust to our decision.

Pam

It's been five years since April was born and I have never regretted our decision to keep her and raise her ourselves.

Barbara

REGRETS?

I have no regrets about the adoption, but it hurts to think of her and many times when I look into those eyes of our new little Erica, I still see the image of Maria.

Warren

One of the questions new parents frequently ask is, "Do you have any regrets about your decision?" Most parents don't express "regrets." Most commonly, parents who chose adoption say they feel "sad." Although many of the parents in this book occasionally question if they wouldn't be more able to cope now that the grief has eased, none would reconsider their decision. All agree that the decision was made with a great deal of pain and effort and with the firm belief that the decision was right for them and their child. Those who chose adoption would not consider disrupting the lives of their child and the child's new family or the lives of their own families to try to reverse a decision so painstakingly made.

Parents Talk

Responses to the question: "Do you have any regrets?"

No. Not at all. I've learned from this experience that people should not be so judgmental about other people. Most people who try to judge me haven't walked in my shoes so they shouldn't tell me not to give up my child. They don't know what they would do unless they are in the position.

Kathleen

NO!!!!

Beth

No—I know that I could never be excited about raising a child with Down syndrome.

Lorraine

Right now I can say no without hesitation. But until I had another child of my own, I always fantasized that maybe I could have physically and emotionally raised a child with such a severe disability.

Lexie

None. I have two more beautiful children and another on the way who would have never had a chance at life if I had kept Matthew.

Trudy

Sometimes. But with a split decision to start, it's to be expected. I feel that if the four of us were together now that there would be a lot of fighting and ill feelings toward each other.

Ann

No. I feel totally confident in the choice I made. It still hurts but I know it was the right choice.

Kevin

No. April has turned out to be a delightful little girl. She is far more capable than we had imagined. . . . The doctor who told us that the second child with LMBBS in the same family is worse was wrong!

Barbara

Yes. Not having Emily adopted privately.

Jeff

Sadness, yes—regrets, never. I am positive we made the right decision for everybody involved—us, Emily, the adoptive family. I have never even considered changing my mind.

Jan

Dave and I are comfortable talking about Jake whenever the need arises. We have both expressed that we have no regrets about our decision, but we are both saddened that we couldn't convince ourselves that we could raise Jake and still have our marriage and the rest of our lives intact.

Randy

Rick and I know we made the right choice. Lanier is a part of our family and he is where he belongs. I cannot imagine how I could justify giving him to another set of parents. I would have never had any inner peace and, for me, that's essential to the quality of my life.

Mary

There are moments when I have regrets but I go through thinking about the process and I don't feel regretful. I wish it had never happened to me but it did. Nobody acknowledges that it's something some of us can't do as well as others.

Rona

Since I really do think we made the right decision I do not regret the decision. I do get pangs of sorrow when I think about it. After all, it is a loss. Maybe I regretted acting this way or saying that, but not anymore. The feeling that can creep up on you is guilt, and it's hard to get rid of guilt even when it becomes inappropriate.

Max

No, but I've never stopped feeling bad about the whole tragedy happening. I will always wish that things could have been different. . . . We feel we did the best thing for him. We learned from our research that he would excel to his most potential only if we were into it, otherwise, he would feel it and know. Every time I see a picture or speak to his adoptive mom, I know he's loved and they give 100 percent of themselves emotionally to him. I could have given him materialistically but not as much emotionally. Adam is with a big family and three other boys with Down syndrome like himself. . . . Either way, whether we kept him or gave him up, it was terribly sad and always will be.

Lauren

No regrets, but we do wonder why we could not raise this baby and other couples can. It will be our ongoing mystery in life. . . . It was not like I could say, well let me bring the baby home and see if we could handle it. I think this would be a very selfish act. I have made the couple who adopted my baby very happy and we think of the three of them often.

Eileen

There are times when I feel sad because I can't afford to buy her clothes or worry if I'll have enough food to feed her all month, but I know the food I'll get for her and the clothes she has we can get by with. I know she's happy, she's fed, she's dry, and she's loved. She's doing the best she can and that's really good. When I look at her in her crib every night I know for me I did the right thing. I know she's with the "perfect" family even with all our imperfections. I especially know my decision was right when she gives me her hugs and kisses, when she brightens up at the sight of her dad or her sisters. I don't think I could ever regret my decision.

Cathie

I will always have regrets about our decision. I will always wonder if I could have taken Nina home and taken care of her. In the back of my mind I realize what a sacrifice this would have been, how different our lives would be.

Pam

No regrets, but we will always wonder what life would be like if we had raised our child ourselves. So far the events that have taken place since we released our child for adoption have only convinced us more that we did make the right decision for us.

Mary Ann and Hank

As I recovered from the grief and felt stronger, I sometimes thought "We could have done it." But it usually only takes a call to the adoptive mom who always sounds so thrilled and so much in love with Brian to set my mind at ease. Our decision was best for all of us and I truly believe that this is the way things were meant to be.

Joanne

FUTURE PREGNANCIES

> Having another child as soon as possible is truly what heals your soul and gives you hope and happiness once again. When my son was born and I counted his ten fingers and toes and took him home was when I began the healing process; till then it was all superficial.
>
> Lexie

Many new parents need to see the whole picture before making a choice. One question frequently asked is, "Will I be able to have more, healthy children if I choose adoption for this baby?"

Most parents who have given birth to a baby with a disability are, understandably, nervous about the prospect of another pregnancy. Most also want to have more children. Lorraine, pregnant again after choosing adoption for her baby with Down syndrome, stated, "I'm scared, but I want Robert to grow up with a brother or sister. I feel like he was cheated, too, through this whole thing."

Parents are usually given information about future risks of having another child with a disability at the same time that the news is given about their baby's disability. It's difficult to process so much information in such a short time while in a state of grief and confusion. The information presented at that time may be forgotten or misunderstood. It is advisable for parents to seek out information from a genetic counselor when their minds are clearer and when they might be more receptive to the information.

A genetic counselor is a specialist who will gather medical history and information about family background, evaluate chromosomal studies of the baby and in some cases do chromosomal studies of both parents. He or she will assess this information to indicate what risks there might be in future pregnancies. This counselor also can offer current information about the prenatal tests that are available and the risks involved in those tests. There are also books available that describe the testing and the risks involved (see resources in the appendix).

There are no guarantees in a pregnancy, as all of the families in this book learned. Having lived through this experience, one may be better able to predict what one would do in the future, but decisions often are not made until the situation presents itself. Most parents who have chosen adoption for a child say that they would receive, or have received, some kind of prenatal test in the next pregnancy. Jan would choose a chorionic villus sample (CVS): "I could not even consider a second-trimester abortion, so amnio would be useless to me." Lorraine did choose to have a CVS during her next pregnancy: "I couldn't live through another shock like that." Lauren chose early amniocentesis, in her seventeenth week of pregnancy. Mary, who cherishes her son, Lanier, chose to have an early amnio when pregnant with her next child: "My OB suggested that I have it because Lanier had not been full-term because of placenta deprivation caused by the chromosomal problem, an extremely serious complication." During the pregnancy she stated, "We had a two-week wait before we got the results of the amnio. It seemed like two years and we were very troubled the entire two weeks. We were, and are, so grateful that we didn't have to make such a decision and that our next baby will be healthy, from a chromosomal standpoint."

Not many parents who chose adoption would consider raising a child with the same disability at a future time. Many parents feel fairly confident that, if there were a diagnosis of the same, or similar, disability, they would abort. The reasons vary. Some feel that the medical problems their first baby had, and the lifesaving techniques, were just too painful for the child. They would not want to give birth to another child with these problems. Trudy has had three pregnancies since Matthew's birth. "I have had amnio with every one. I am Catholic and am against abortion for the purpose of just not wanting a baby, but after going through what we went through with Matthew, I would never subject another infant to what he has to face, not only the Down syndrome, but his severe heart problems." Other parents know the pain they went through with the "letting go" and want to protect themselves. Jan, not yet pregnant again, stated, "I would have CVS and I would abort. I couldn't raise a disabled child, and I couldn't give away another baby. I know it would be extremely difficult, and I'm sure I would feel guilty, but I would do it anyway." A few parents so adamantly oppose abortion that they would continue the pregnancy, but would choose adoption again. Dan and Beth do not want more children. Beth is opposed to abortion and shared, "If I did become pregnant again I would want to know if the baby were normal or not. If not normal, I would know now to make plans to adopt but still would not abort." Some parents just pray that the choice won't have to be made, because they don't know what they would do. Joanne couldn't decide if she wanted to become pregnant again. "It took me over a year after Brian's birth to reach the decision that if I were to become pregnant again, I would choose to have a CVS and that I *think* I would abort if it showed a chromosomal problem."

For most parents, the prenatal testing is just reassurance that the baby will not have certain disabilities and most do go on to have more, healthy children. The pregnancy following the one with a result of a disability is not easy. Most mothers, and fathers, live in a state of fear until after the test results. Then, though they feel some comfort that the child does not have a disability that can be detected through prenatal testing, they worry about all of the other possible complications. In the seventh month of pregnancy, one mother stated, "I won't feel relieved until this child is walking and talking."

Many parents who choose adoption want to get pregnant soon after the child has gone to live with his or her new family. Other parents caution that although having another baby helps, it does not replace the loss. Jan advises, "Mourning the loss of your baby is extremely painful and it takes time. I just wanted it to be over—I couldn't stand the pain anymore. I wanted to have another baby immediately to replace Emily, but I also realized that I was just trying to avoid the necessary and inevitable mourning process—a process that couldn't be rushed or cheated."

Mothers also should consider both their physical and emotional health. A woman must be physically healthy to sustain a pregnancy. Some women have experienced difficulty getting pregnant again, and still others have miscarried soon after becoming pregnant. Mary Ann had a miscarriage nine months after her baby with Down syndrome was born: "That really depressed me even more and for a long time. Anxiety may have been a major factor in the length of time for me to become pregnant again." It would be advisable for mothers to have a checkup with their obstetrician before attempting to get pregnant again.

The grieving process takes time and the emotional health of the mother must be a major consideration before attempting another pregnancy. The scheduling of the prenatal testing procedures and the time spent waiting for results is often a period of anxiety. If there should be an abnormal result, or a miscarriage, the parents, especially the mother, must be prepared psychologically to deal with the consequences. Joanne relates:

Everyone else seemed to be getting pregnant right away [after choosing adoption]. I waited two years. When I became pregnant, I found the whole ordeal of scheduling the tests to be emotionally exhausting. Then when I miscarried, I was so glad I'd waited. I couldn't have dealt with the emotions even six months sooner.

Parents Talk

I had a healthy baby boy thirteen months after the birth of our baby with Down syndrome. Our new baby, Seth, is my blessing. He has made life go on for my family and especially for me. . . . The memory isn't as strong in my mind as time goes on because of my Seth. If the amniocentesis had shown Down syndrome, I would have terminated the pregnancy without thinking twice. I really believe that people who refuse amnio or CVS are willing to accept and keep any baby born to them.

Lauren

With Lanier's pregnancy, there was no reason to do an amnio because I was only 32 and already had three normal children. The whole thing was taken out of my hands and I'm glad it was. When I found out I was pregnant again, you can imagine the fear I experienced. The pain I went through last August, realizing that Lanier had an extra chromosome, his two-month hospital stay, the emergency birth via C-section, was almost more than I could bear. Then, the decision-making process was a lot to hold up under. . . . After my husband and I thought about it, we felt that we really needed to know if the baby I was carrying was chromosomally healthy or not. . . . We would look down at Lanier when he was asleep and he was so precious and peaceful, or we'd just melt when he would reach up his tiny hands to grab our faces—how could we terminate what would become a human life? It was a tough consideration and, thank God, we got normal results. We continue to pray that this baby will be healthy and that we can experience the joy and jubilation that comes from having a normal, healthy baby.

Mary

[Mary and Rick gave birth to a healthy son two months after she wrote this.]

What happened to us is not detectable unless you suspect it and look for its effects. . . . It is a mutation of a gene, not an aberration of a chromosome. . . . Unless it happened once to you, you are certainly not likely to suspect it, and you probably wouldn't even think of it.

We could not make a decision about a future pregnancy until Rona's two medications were tapered and discontinued. When it was clear my wife was better, handling stresses—routine and not so routine—we checked our decision. We knew it could generate irrational fears. We also knew the facts about recurrence rates but we felt we could provide a great home and growing up experience for another child. . . . The chance of achondroplasia happening again is the same as the first time, that is, very small.

Max

Prenatal diagnosis can't detect everything. There can be false results. Weird things can still happen. I had had an ultrasound at twelve weeks to confirm dates, an ultrasound again at twenty weeks and amniocentesis [during the pregnancy in which I carried Naomi] with no abnormalities showing.

For the next pregnancy, I went to Yale for serial detailed ultrasonography—twice. I would have gone to California, if that were the only place to get it! I would have aborted anytime up until the date for legal abortion.

Rona

[Max and Rona gave birth to a healthy son in May 1991.]

After the birth of the baby with Down syndrome and then the miscarriage, I continued to feel depressed and anxious, until I was about seven months pregnant at which time I began to feel that maybe everything would be OK this time. This was about one-and-a-half years in length. I was afraid we wouldn't be able to have any more children, but we did have two more and they bring us so much joy. It's so much easier now to "count our blessings" and be happy for our child with Down syndrome and his adoptive family. With both pregnancies we had prenatal diagnosis and probably would have chosen abortion if there had been a chromosomal defect.

Mary Ann

Had I been offered the amniocentesis during my pregnancy with Maria, I probably would have chosen to have it done for my own peace of mind. If ever I had a fear, it would have been to have a baby born with Down syndrome. My doctor didn't feel it was necessary because I was only 34 with no past history of any disabilities. . . . If the doctors are sure that there is a problem [with this pregnancy], I will definitely terminate the pregnancy.

Lorraine

[Lorraine and Warren gave birth to a healthy daughter eight months after writing this.]

I want to have another baby because if I don't I will just sit around and think of things that could go wrong. I will have amnio and would probably abort if there was a chromosomal problem.

Kathleen

[Kathleen and Bob gave birth to a healthy boy a year after Laura was born.]

Dave and I considered amniocentesis when I was pregnant with Jake. We talked about it, but were afraid of causing a possible miscarriage. We specifically talked about the "what if" we have a baby with Down syndrome and rather quickly concluded that with our backgrounds in working with emotionally disturbed children, we'd be OK. We know now that we barely scratched the surface, but I'm glad I didn't have to deal with making an abortion decision. That, too, would have been a real loss and tragedy.

We've just had another healthy, normal, baby boy. I chose to have a CVS and probably would have had an abortion if the test had shown Down syndrome.

Randy

One of the things which angered me most during the months following Brian's birth was the societal acceptance of abortion, but not of adoption, especially among the members of the medical profession. The attitude seemed to be that if I hadn't wanted to raise my son, I should have had amnio, which I had refused. Given the ignorance in this community about adoption and our own feelings of incompetency, I would have had to choose abortion without knowing there were other options.

Joanne

[Joanne became pregnant two years after Brian's birth. She miscarried before the scheduled CVS appointment.]

We want to adopt again and pray that we can.

Julie

I plan to have a baby to raise as soon as possible. I started trying to conceive when Emily was 10 months old. Six months later I'm still not pregnant. Part of me is afraid I'll never be able to get pregnant again or that I'll never produce a normal baby. After all, I'm 32 years old and don't have a normal baby yet. An-

other part of me knows that this is irrational, that I have a good chance of having a normal baby. Still, as I certainly found out, there are no guarantees in life.

Jan

[Jan became pregnant in 1991. Prenatal tests, CVS and MSAFP, were normal. A healthy son was born in March 1992.]

At first I didn't want more children. My husband did. I did not want to take the dice of life, throw it against the wall, and have it come up against me again. I was afraid of losing again. I do have my first daughter, but as my husband pointed out she needs a sibling, which got me into trouble to begin with. We will, if we can, and I'll be scared the entire nine months.

Eileen

[Eileen and Louis gave birth to a healthy son ten months after she wrote this, and a daughter two years later.]

At first I said that I didn't even want to try to have any more children but now I'm starting to think that maybe someday we will.

Kevin

I do want another baby but Kevin isn't too sure about it at this point. [If I do get pregnant] I will have testing done. With no hesitation I would abort the baby. I don't ever want to relinquish another child to someone else.

Ann

Throughout the pregnancy with Sara, I carried very small. I always questioned my size and the doctor said, "Consider yourself lucky." I had no testing.

I've had two more children, a boy and a girl, since Sara's birth. . . . I had testing done with the future pregnancies and would terminate without a doubt. My decision required so much soul-searching. I now know I cannot care for a child with severe needs. In essence taking a test is for that reason—to carry full term or not—there is no in between anymore.

Lexie

I don't want any more children, not because of Angela but because I'm too old. I already have four children and that's enough. I never want to go through what I did before either. . . . I would have prenatal diagnosis again [if I became pregnant] just to be prepared. I'm positive I would have the baby and raise the child.

Cathie

An amnio would not have revealed Nicole's particular condition. I had no reason to believe that we would have anything other than a normal child.

I did have amnio with my third child. It came out fine and this gave me some peace of mind, but, as I said, Nicole's was a genetic, but not a chromosomal problem, so an amnio would not have detected another child with her syndrome. I was 36 years old when I became pregnant with our son, so I would have had an amnio even if Nicole wasn't born with disabilities.

Sue

Two years after Nina was born I did become pregnant. However, I lost the baby during the first three months. In April 1985, we had a healthy baby girl. My husband and I both had genetic testing done before the pregnancy. I did have an amniocentesis while I was pregnant with my third child. If I had a similar diagnosis there is no doubt in my mind that I would have had an abortion. Throughout the many hospital stays our daughter has had, I have seen many children suffer with different prognoses. I do not feel children should be brought in this world to suffer.

Pam

I had a tubal ligation performed immediately after April's delivery. . . . I would definitely have prenatal diagnosis again and if there were an abnormal diagnosis I would start from square one again and make the best decision I could based on what I know now. . . . I can't say for sure that I would keep the baby or even continue the pregnancy. It depends on so many factors. . . . It's hard to say what we would have done had Damon been diagnosed with LMBBS prenatally. I probably would have read what the medical journals had to say about the syndrome and consulted a few doctors about what to do, and I just may have decided to opt for an abortion. I might not have thought to try to talk with the parents of a child with the syndrome or actually meet a child with it.

Barbara

Note to New Parents _____

Life does return to a new normal. You will smile, and even laugh, again—without acting. You will find pleasure again doing activities you used to enjoy. You will love your other children as wholeheartedly as you did before. You probably will even find yourself annoyed by "little" things again.

If you desire to have another child, you will find a time that's right and you will make it through whatever prenatal testing you choose. No one enjoys another pregnancy, but most parents do go on to have at least one more healthy child. There can be happiness in your future, but it will take time.

All Because of You

What were you thinking the last time
you stood above me looking down?
Did it hurt to say "good-bye"
to these two eyes of brown?
How could you let go of me
if you loved me?
Was it so I could learn to live
and be all that I could be?
Sometimes I lie awake and wonder
how my life would have changed
If I had grown up as someone else
with another name.
I think of how you would have been
if you were still alive.
I have so many things to ask—
I wish you hadn't died.
I cannot change what happened,
nor would I want to.
I have a family who loves me,
all because of you.
I wish you could see me,
and what I have become.
If you could, you would be pleased,
all thanks to my Mom,
The woman who has raised me
for seventeen years.
Who has listened to my dreams
and wiped away my tears.
She has made me who I am
instead of another.
She is the only woman
who I can call "Mother."
If I had the chance to talk to you,
I'd have to say "Thank you."
I have a family who loves me—
all because of you.

Angela Grafstrom

Dedicated to Jean "Sissy" Evans (1/14/59–8/8/76). Angela has spina bifida. She was adopted at 14 months. Her birthmother died when she was 2 years old.

10

Final Messages

MESSAGES

> Make sure you tell them . . .
>
> Everyone interviewed

The families interviewed had so much to say. Many were anxious to get messages to medical professionals. Experiences varied, but some parents had such uncomfortable interactions with doctors, nurses, or social workers that they wanted an opportunity to offer words of advice in hopes of paving a smoother road for future new parents. Some parents were not given an opportunity to leave a letter for their child or to say a proper goodbye. Some never met the adoptive families or had the occasion to let them know how grateful they are. All wanted to offer a word of support for new parents. This final chapter offers these messages. Though intended for specific audiences, all readers will be enlightened by reading these words. The last section of this chapter summarizes the story of each family as they offer words of comfort to new parents.

PARENT MESSAGES TO MEDICAL PROFESSIONALS

> When you speak to parents you must remember above all else that they are delicate, fragile, and emotional. . . . Parents and children and that relationship of love is precious and should be handled with care.
>
> Julie

Professionals walk a tightrope when dealing with parents who are grief-stricken. Anger that is part of the grieving process often is directed at these professionals who deliver the shocking news. Professionals need to respect that new parents are in a vulnerable position. Far too often professionals let personal biases affect the support and care they give the families. Often, parents interviewed were supported initially, but as it became clear that adoption was being seriously considered, personal opinions sometimes interfered with professionalism. Parents who received caring help from medical professionals greatly appreciated the unbiased support. The following messages are intended to help professionals cope with parents both initially and later, as parents explore options.

Parents Talk

Don't just fix the physical ills. The emotional ones are a lot stronger.

Trudy

Take more of an interest in the person, not just do the job. Follow up and be more concerned with the patient's state of mind.

Lauren and Michael

Be compassionate, put yourself in others' shoes. Get out of your "clinical" mode and become a real and empathetic person. Listen to yourself. There is a way to present bad news in a respectful and thoughtful manner. If you can't handle it well, get someone who can. Also have a priest, minister, or caring counselor on hand to be there.

Julie

Be objective and nonjudgmental about a decision being made by a family to give their child up for adoption. No one knows what it feels like being faced with raising a handicapped child unless you've walked that road, too.

Lorraine and Warren

Try to realize what a parent goes through while making these decisions. It's not an easy task.

Kevin

I think the doctors should try to put themselves in our shoes. I feel because I chose adoption, I chose life for my son, not death. I also feel that they are supposed to give knowledge of medicine and facts, but what I initially saw was judge, jury, and executioner.

Ann

Provide updated information. Every case is different, so don't assume anything. Present all the options early on. Be honest, realistic, and supportive of the parents' decision.

Mary Ann and Hank

My hope is that members of this [medical] "community" are not so cold, distant, and uncomfortable with this type of tragedy.

Jeff

Keep your judgments to yourself. You're not trained, qualified, paid, or needed to dispense your personal moral agenda to people in tragic and painful situations. Offer honest information, at least, and nonjudgmental support—if you are able to.

Jan

Do not be judgmental. Personal preferences have no place when one is trying to be objective in helping people make a choice that is right for them.

Max

Be more in touch with reality. The news you are delivering may not be a big deal to some people, but to others it is. Get more in touch with the parents' feelings.

Rona

Parents need help tapping into resources whether or not they keep or give up their baby. If parents are requesting information about options, have the information available. Written information and a support system needs to be at least offered to the parents.

If it's apparent that the parents are not coping, then it needs to be brought to the attention of the head of nursing. It is not helpful to bide the time away for three days thinking that, "Oh, well, in a couple of days she'll be going home with the baby and it's no longer our problem."

A grieving counselor would be appropriate in many cases, with followup after the mother leaves the hospital.

Randy and Dave

Don't be so quick to suggest terminating pregnancies. You need to have more information available, more updated materials. You don't have to paint a devastating picture. Add some of the positive, not just the negative. Put parents in contact with other parents who have been through this. Rather than suggesting abortion, let the parents know that there is a waiting list of parents who want to adopt special needs children.

Cathie

Please put aside all your personal feelings at a time like this. If you don't know how to help, find a medical person with the right background who can.

Lexie

I was really angry after I read the medical records on our daughter. A physician must be compassionate in a personal tragedy such as this. Please do not make judgments on parents' behalf and on how you feel they should be reacting to the situation. The first seven years of our daughter's life were pure hell. We were fearful of every single call we received late at night, and on the nights we had to rush to the hospital and make life-threatening decisions. We had to see our daughter suffer through every single illness, seizure, surgery, wondering every time if this was her last. How can you possibly know the feeling of parents at each passing birthday? . . .

Listen to what your patient is trying to tell you. . . . If something does not sound right, pursue the matter more. If testing is performed and there is the slightest doubt that something could be wrong, please go further with the situation. Please take the time to listen!!!!

Pam

Don't judge. Try and get the whole story. Think before you speak. Try to be a little human—that's why you're in the field you're in—to help others.

Eileen and Louis

Be as unbiased and unopinionated as possible in dealing with the subject of handicapped fetuses, abortion, and adoption. As long as abortion is legal, it is a viable choice for many women; . . . the same thing goes for adoption. If someone chooses not to raise a child, then adoption should be a viable choice for that woman/couple. And if a woman or couple decide to keep their handicapped child, that too is a viable option. Regardless of the outcome, these decisions should be given the same amount of respect and support. Try to abstain from giving unsolicited, personal advice.

Barbara

We don't really have any messages. We had excellent experiences with the doctors and nurses. They went way out of their way to comfort, reassure, show concern, and offer help anytime we needed it.

However, the social worker assigned to us was unhelpful, insensitive, and tried to help but was condescending, patronizing, and generally irritating. She didn't do the paperwork we needed right away. We had to find out about Rachel's developmental care by ourselves.

Beth and Daniel

Please be honest with the parents from the start. Don't try to "sugarcoat" the situation for the parents' sake. If we had known for sure a year ago that Nicole was mentally retarded, we may have made this decision sooner. The older she gets, the harder it is going to be on everyone involved when we finally have to relinquish her.

Sue

Offer information. Parents should be aware of amniocentesis and allowed to make choices about having the test. Give information to parents about why this happens and what options there are.

Kathleen

Parents in a state of grief need someone who will listen and who will give support in whatever they are thinking or feeling. Be sensitive to the individuals in the family. Have knowledge of options available. Try to withhold judgment should the family be considering an option other than one you think you would choose yourself. Get to know the parents before you offer any advice, and then choose your words carefully.

Joanne

MESSAGES FROM BIRTHPARENTS TO ADOPTIVE PARENTS

Dear Stephanie,
  Thank you! Thank you! Thank you! Thank you!

Love, Beth

Birthparents who have closed adoptions seldom have an opportunity to offer words of thanks to adoptive parents. Even those with open adoptions do not always have an occasion to express feelings. Though these messages may not be identified by the adoptive families of the particular child, hopefully the words will convey the feelings of birthparents to all adoptive families.

Parents Talk

In a letter I wrote to the adoptive family a few months ago, I basically told them how happy I was that things were going so well. I told them that we were getting on with our lives and that we have no regrets of our decision, only regrets that we couldn't convince ourselves we could raise Jake. I wished them all happiness on his first birthday and enclosed some birth photos for them. I thanked them for adopting and loving Jake and assured them that we wouldn't interfere.

Randy

I would like to tell the family that we want them to give our child a lot of love, caring, and understanding. Don't think ill of us because we gave our child up. Some people were just made to accept limitations of these children better than others.

Michael

I would like to thank the family. I am indebted to them for wanting Adam. I would tell them to give him lots of love, kiss him for me. God bless them. They're wonderful people, saints from heaven.

Lauren

To the prospective adoptive family:
  Please love our little girl like she were your own, and give her the support that we could not give her.

Sue

I wrote a letter asking them to love and cherish her as if she were their own. I told them how bad we felt and how much we loved her ourselves, but we knew she would be in a much happier home than ours could ever be.

Lorraine

I would tell them how happy I am that they are willing and able to give Michael what he needs. I would tell them that they are very special people and that they are caring for a very special person. I would thank them for doing something that I couldn't do.

Kevin

Thank you for giving our son love and a home to grow up in.

Ann

Thank you for taking good care of Laura and giving her a chance at life and supporting her emotionally. I can't thank you enough.

Kathleen

Thank you. We pray for you always. We're happy the child has been able to bring joy into your life.

Mary Ann and Hank

At times I envy your ability to love my son more unconditionally than I ever could. I'm jealous that you will see each accomplishment and experience this joy. But, I'm ever so grateful that you chose to parent him and that you share so freely with me the stories of his growth. He is yours as much as any child can "belong" to his parents and I find comfort, and peace, in knowing how much you love him and how well you care for him. Thank you.

Joanne

If our child realizes she was adopted and asks of us, please speak good of us. You were adopted yourself, so you know how it feels. Tell her this. Tell her your circle is complete. Let her grow to her fullest potential. Have patience with her, but we know you will. Tell her we love her very much, but we could not raise her. Keep her happy. You all are in our prayers every day.

Eileen and Louis

I keep in touch with the adoptive family on a regular basis. We both write about everything—everyday things, our personal thoughts, et cetera.

Trudy

Thank you.
Thank you for your love . . .
Thank you for your strength . . .
Thank you for your wisdom . . .
Our utmost and deepest gratitude toward you and your family.

Lexie

I wrote to the family through a mutual contact in the Down syndrome parent support group. I asked for an annual "update" and photo and the family denied the request.

Jan

We thank you sincerely for taking our daughter, Nina, into your home and giving her the love and care she needs. . . . You have taken care of her when she has been released from the hospital in serious condition. You are there to take care of her every need. . . . We could never repay you for all that you have done. I hope that you understand how Nina affects us mentally and emotionally. I would always be in despair or feeling sorry for her. I look at Nina very differently than you do. To this day I cannot say I accept what has happened. . . . I hope you will someday understand the pain we have gone through, the marriage and financial difficulties. . . . I would like to have done more for Nina and you. . . . We can never express how grateful we are that you are Nina's family care providers.

Pam

Dear family,
There are many things we wish to say to you. We thank you very much for "being there." Some things are easier for some people and some things are more difficult. We found that we are not able to cope with this situation and this realization grieves us. We want the best for Naomi and we believe we cannot provide that for her and you can do it better.

Good luck and good health,
Naomi's birthparents

BIRTHPARENTS' MESSAGES TO THEIR CHILDREN

I will always love you even though I cannot be with you. You are forever in my mind as well as my heart.

Ann

Many parents felt that their children with disabilities, especially those with mental retardation, would never understand adoption, or birth/ adoptive parents, so chose not to write a message to their children. One father stated, "It hurts too much to do this, I'm sorry."

Parents Talk

I'll always have a special place in my heart for you and will love you in my own way. I'm sorry that I couldn't convince myself that you and I could be happy in our family forever more. I'm sorry nature did this to you. I want you to know that we searched very hard to find a wonderful family for you.

Randy

I hope I made the best decision for you.

Kathleen

I have written a long letter to Hollie. It is not done—there is so much to say. I write to her in my mind daily: "I love you my darling. I'm so sorry this happened to you. Please understand. I love you always."

Julie

Dear Rachel,
Dear little one, you cannot help how you have been made. I am sorry that I don't have the strength to stand by your side through your life and help you cope. You have now the best mommy in the world. We thank God for her and that you truly are her Rachel Joy.

Love, your birth mommy and daddy (Beth and Daniel)

God bless you and look over you always.

Warren

To Adam: We will always think of you and love and feel sorry about everything that happened. Why couldn't it have turned out differently? Why? Why? Why? We gave you up to a family that will be able to accept you and be happy for you for all that you can accomplish in life, what we thought to be the best decision for everyone!

Michael

Dear Brian,
Your name has been changed, but you will always be "my" Brian. I hope you someday understand that your mommy and daddy who care for you love you very much and that the mommy and daddy who gave you life love you just as much, only in a different way. We chose to give you life and then felt that you needed to live where you would be provided with the love and care to become the best you could ever be. I'm sorry that we couldn't do that for you, but you have a wonderful family who can.

Love, Your other mommy (Joanne)

We love you, precious daughter of ours. Speak to your mom if you don't understand something. She will help you understand, for she is a special lady. I was glad to have given birth to you. Just make your mom and dad proud of you, which I don't doubt for a moment you will. Baby, just remember, your birth mom and dad love you very much, honestly, cross our broken hearts.

Eileen

I would try to explain to Michael why I made the choices that I did. I would tell him how much it hurt to do what I did but it was done with his best interests in mind. I would tell him that I love him.

Kevin

I love you very much, and always will. I would love to see you if you want to see me. I gave you up because I couldn't be the kind of mother you need or give

you the family you deserve. I gave you to your new family because I knew that
you would be better taken care of and happier with them.

Jan

To Nicole:
You are a precious little girl. We love you very much. Please forgive us for not
being strong enough to raise you. We gave you up out of love. We will think of
you every day for the rest of our lives. We will always be your mommy and
daddy.

Sue

Dear Daughter,
You stayed with us for the first three months of your life. . . . You were a
wonderful and beautiful baby. . . . Once we learned about your prospective adoptive family, it seemed clear that they were more capable of giving you emotional
support and the way to a good life than we were. Your father and I searched our
hearts and souls, and with great difficulty decided that it would be better for all
of us if you were raised by your adoptive parents. . . .
Dear Daughter, . . . we are your biologic parents, but being a parent is more
than creating a conceptus. Your real parents are those who, unconditionally, care
for you when you are sick, have fed you, clothed you, and sought you out to
complete and enrich their lives. Please understand that we made our decision
with love.
You'll always be in my heart and thoughts.

I love you,
Mother

(excerpt from the letter Rona provided for Naomi)

Dear Daughter,
Please know that we hope that our decision, made with love, will allow you to
flourish. It makes me sad to know that we could not provide for you the environment that you deserve. I wish you health, happiness, and success.

Love,
Your father

(excerpt from the letter Max provided for Naomi)

FINAL MESSAGES

Feelings are neither right nor wrong. They just are.
Lynn (adoptive mom)

These final messages offered are especially for new parents, yet all
readers can find words of wisdom from these parents who have walked a
long, difficult, lonely road. All families have survived the turmoil; marriages are still intact. All have gone on with their lives. Though some
have taken longer to recover, each is healing in their own time. Many

speak in terms of "before" and "after" the birth of their child with a disability. The experience has left each one different, viewing life in a different way.

Lorraine and Warren considered adoption soon after they received word of Maria's disabilities, but didn't make the final decision until she was 2 months old. The adoption took place when Maria was 3 months old.

Lorraine says, "I think of my baby everyday, but time has healed some of the pain. I thank the Lord there are people out there who are willing to adopt a child like this. I knew I could never be this type of person."

Warren says, "I feel that my prayers were answered by finding a loving family to accept and love a child with a handicap who I emotionally was unable to accept. In my heart I feel the decision was best."

Kathleen, who chose guardianship, says, "It [alternative care] is probably the best thing you can do for the child as well as the rest of the family. I feel that the rest of my family would have suffered. It would have taken from my other kids and from my marriage if I were to help my child with Down syndrome reach her full potential.

"It takes a bigger person to admit that you can't handle raising a child like this than it does to bring them home and then pretend and just go through the motions. I was honest with myself from the beginning and I knew that I could not raise a child like this. This does not make me a bad person. I think that I'm a better person for making the sacrifice of giving up my baby so she will have a better life than I could give her. She will reach her full potential with her new family."

Lexie and Scott made the decision that Sara would be adopted when she was 4 weeks old. After they signed the adoption papers, they were asked to stop calling the intensive care unit to check up on her. They found out later, via Lexie's therapist, that Sara had been adopted.

Lexie's message for new parents: "Remember that you have to grow old with your child—babies grow up and become adults and this is when the sacrifice, work, and heartache set in. So do what is right for you and ignore others' judgments, because when they leave and go home to their happy homes you still have your problems. What*ever* you choose is right for *you!* Neither choice is easy, but whatever choice you make, it's the right one for you and your family."

Mary Ann and Hank took Adam home; after four weeks of educating themselves, they used foster care. Adam went from foster care to the adoptive family. The adoption became final when Adam was 18 months old.

Mary Ann and Hank advise new parents: "You, and any other children you may have, are the only ones who have to live with your decision. Don't let anyone else pressure you into doing something you feel in your heart isn't in your or your child's best interests. Neither decision, keeping the child or releasing the child, is 'right' or 'wrong,' but one of them is 'best' for you and your family."

Sue and Rick were in the process of looking for an adoptive family for Nicole when they were interviewed for this book. It had been two months since their decision to choose an adoption plan for Nicole.

Sue says, "It helped me to find out that I was not alone, and that I was not a horrible person for giving up my child. You are doing what's right for you and, most importantly, for your child. I feel very selfish because when Nicole is adopted it will make our life happier, but it will also, in the long run, make her so much happier than she could have been with us."

Pam and Rich did not bring Nina home from the hospital. She went first to one family care home, later to the home where she currently lives. Pam and Rich still retain legal custody of Nina.

Pam advises: "No matter what the defect is, do some research, get as much information as you can. Try to find a support group. Do not be afraid to ask a lot of questions. Be very persistent with your doctors. No one is ever mentally prepared for a child with a handicap. You must think of your child and your family. . . . Communication must be kept open between you and your spouse. . . . If you really love each other you have to try to work together to make it. . . . The decision has to come from within yourselves. Please do not listen to other people's remarks. *No* one can possibly know what you are going through unless they have been through a similar situation. Do not let anyone make you feel guilty. . . . If you do decide to place your child, you should investigate the state and what it has to offer, your options, and most important the home where your child will be placed."

Jan and Jeff's daughter, Emily, went to live with the adoptive family when she left the hospital. Due to red tape with the public service agency that handled the paperwork, the adoption was not finalized until fourteen months later.

Jan advises new parents: "Get a clear, realistic picture of what it is to raise a disabled child. Read books, speak to others who have raised a disabled child *through adulthood*. Don't romanticize. Don't use the word 'should'—'I should be able to . . .'; 'I should care enough to . . .'; et cetera. Be brutally honest with yourself, accept all of your feelings. Get professional help if needed. Don't listen to people who are trying to persuade you towards either side of the decision.

"While it never goes away, and it changes your life forever, the pain of losing a baby does become less acute, does become bearable in time. If you choose adoption, once you are past the most intense phase, after a few months, make the time, find the money, and make it a priority to get away on a vacation with your spouse. It is extremely therapeutic, healing, revitalizing, and helps you see that you can still have joy and pleasure in your life."

Julie and Lee's decision to choose an adoption plan for Hollie was made when Hollie was 12 months old. Hollie lived with them for fifteen-and-a-half months.

They offer to parents making the decision: "It is important that you look into your heart to know and understand your limitations even if those limitations mean you must be apart from one another. You must think of the best for your child and for your lives—even if it means those lives be separate."

Lauren and Michael had Adam home for three weeks while they took time to research Down syndrome and the care Adam would need. They felt they were the wrong parents for Adam and that he would be better off with a family who could accept his limitations and the future.

Michael's advice to new parents: "I think the first thing that comes to mind when one considers putting their child up for adoption is guilt—the guilt of not wanting their own child. I think parents considering this option need support that they are doing what they feel is right for *them*. It is their decision, something no one else can even begin to understand as far as feelings, emotions, et cetera. Support groups to help parents cope and survive these extremely tough times would be key!"

Max and Rona had Naomi home with them for three months before she went to live with her adoptive family. They offer for new parents: "You must do what in your heart and brain (emotional and analytical parts of your mind) make sense to you. Weigh the plusses and minuses of all options. Much you can never know. Communicate with your spouse. Neither shoulder all the responsibility nor abdicate your place as decision maker, at least not in the long run. When it's done, don't go back and make a different decision, don't doubt yourself. Take the ball and run with it. Mourn and suffer bereavement. Then get better and get back to life because that is what it's all about."

Trudy and Rick's son, Matthew, was in the hospital for two months of the first four months of his life. During Matthew's frequent episodes of hospitalization, Trudy became friends with a woman who had adopted a child with Down syndrome. When Trudy came to the realization that she couldn't parent Matthew, this woman and her family agreed to adopt Matthew.

Trudy's message to new parents: "If given the chance, speak to other parents who have had to face the decision and speak with people who have chosen different routes, both giving up the child and keeping him.

The parents are the real professionals in this situation, not the doctors or the therapists."

Rick and Mary brought Lanier home for two weeks, after which time he went to stay with a potential adoptive family. The adoptive family was willing to give the birthparents two weeks' time to decide if the adoption would go through and become permanent. However, after ten days, Rick and Mary realized that adoption was not the answer for them and they took Lanier home.

Mary and Rick say: "Lanier is loved for who he is, a precious baby boy, who laughs, smiles, coos, and responds to everyone and everything around him. He brings us joy and happiness and makes our hearts break open and melt when he accomplishes each developmental task. We know we are doing right by raising him and by helping him reach his full potential."

Mary's message to new parents: "I truly believe that every couple has to make their own decision and that everyone has different strengths. I also really believe that it is not my place to judge others or what they do. I must say that I don't think you can fully appreciate the baby in a few months. Lanier is very special and loving and wears me down with his loving nature and open affection. I am so proud when he masters developmental tasks because he works so hard to do it.

"I pray for any couple who gives birth to a baby with Down syndrome. Your heart just breaks for your baby to have to be different, and perhaps the hardest aspect is that there is no joy or jubilation initially—it has to be learned. These babies also can give joy and happiness; it's just a different ballgame than with normal babies."

Ann and Kevin retained custody of Michael until he was 4 weeks old. He left the hospital to go to live with his new family.

Kevin advises new parents: "I suggest reading anything you can get your hands on. Having a normal child is hard enough when you're new at being parents. Having a special needs child is devastating to say the least, but you do have choices you can make to make the best out of a terrible situation."

Ann offers: "Remember, it's your baby and your decision. Some couples may make their decision in a few hours, or days; others it may take months. You have all the time you need to make a decision that *you* can live with. Your family and friends won't be the ones who will raise your child who will need twenty-four-hour care and numerous doctor appointments. You will and only you."

Beth and Dan thoroughly educated themselves to what Rachel's disabilities would mean to their family and to Rachel and felt they would be prepared to raise her. Beth says, "When we brought her home from ICN, reality (which I thought I had a grasp on) hit me like a tidal wave and I flipped out and couldn't function. I realized that I couldn't do it—that I didn't want to—and I had a pretty good idea of what raising her was going to mean." Dan took six weeks off from work and they went for counseling. About a month later they found Stephanie.

Beth and Daniel offer for new parents: "Call us anytime. We really did our homework on both sides of the decision and can give informed, intelligent help."

Joanne and Bob had Brian at home for six weeks and then Brian lived in foster care until they found the adoptive family. Brian was adopted on his 4-month birthday.

For parents considering adoption Joanne offers: "Think of your child and what you truly believe will be best for him or her. If you firmly believe that someone else can give your child more unconditional love than you feel capable of, then that may be the best choice for you. If you will constantly worry that your baby is not getting proper care, then you will be his best parents. Give yourself time to overcome the grief, to make the decision out of your love for the infant that you have given birth to and not out of grief for the one you lost."

Barbara and Donn decided about one month after the prenatal diagnosis that they would raise their baby. April was born in October 1986. Barbara was "surprised at how pretty and petite she was. Our son was quite a sight at birth . . . but April looked pretty much like any other newborn."

Barbara offers to new parents: "If you have just discovered that the child you have conceived or gave birth to has a handicapping condition, please take time to consider all of your options. Don't rush into making a decision that you may later regret. Get as much information as you can. . . . Try not to focus on the condition so much as the unique individual who happens to be afflicted with a particular condition. It's not easy being the parent of a child with special needs, but then again it's not easy being a parent—period. Children with handicapping conditions need the same things as their nonhandicapped peers—unconditional love and acceptance.

Eileen and Louis chose adoption for Emily when she was 3 weeks old, after visiting schools, talking with social workers, doctors, priests, and other parents. Eileen read books about living with children with disabilities, which helped to confirm her decision.

Eileen says: "I don't think if I'd kept my baby I would ever have another baby. I would be too busy and I would dedicate my life to my baby with Down syndrome. This wouldn't have been fair to my first child. We did a lot of soul-searching and we believe, for us, we made the *best* decision. . . . We realize we would not be the best parents for the child, and that's OK. You just have to try and accept and live with yourself."

Cathie brought Angela home from the hospital even though the adoptive family already had been found and many of the arrangements had been made. Some red tape in the legalities hindered Angela's move to her new family and during this time Cathie made the decision that she couldn't go through with adoption.

Cathie advises new parents: "Find a good therapist, but most of all take your baby home, spend time with your baby, get to know and love your baby. No matter what your final decision, you'll never regret the time you spent with him or her. If you feel at peace with your decision I feel you'll be making the right decision. Give yourself the time to adjust to the news. When you first find out your baby has an abnormality, you almost have to go through a grieving process. You grieve the loss of your normal, healthy baby that you expected. Once you do that you can then start to accept the baby you're going to have or already have.

"Don't be alarmed if you have hours or even a day that you don't want to hold the baby or be near the baby. It's probably your own body's mechanism shutting down to protect you. Most of all don't feel guilty no matter what you're feeling or thinking. You'll more than likely go through every emotion there is during this time. Talk to someone and don't be too hard on yourself. There's a lot of people who have gone through this who would be more than eager to try and help, to listen, to be there for you. You're not alone."

Randy and Dave had Jake home with them for five weeks and then he was in a respite home until the adoption took place when he was 9 weeks old. Randy wrote an article about their experience, which was published in *Working Mother* magazine in September 1989.

Randy offers: "I'd like to let all new parents know how comforting it has been to know that all our personal lives, thoughts, and feelings may reach out and support you during one of the most difficult times of your lives. From this moment on your lives are changed forevermore regardless of your decision. Be honest with everyone. Educate yourself extensively about your baby's disability, including visits to schools and workshops or group homes for adult persons with disabilities. Take your time in making the decision, but, more importantly, make a decision one way or the other rather than live life through indecision. Above all, work through your decision with your spouse and no one else. Don't let anyone pressure you in either direction. I believe that through this careful process your decision will be the best for you. And, yes, you will find peace and happiness again."

Appendix: Resources

INFORMATION ABOUT DISABILITIES

In order to familiarize yourself with your child's disability, you will need to gather information. The following books are offered as a place to start and are not endorsed by the publisher or author of this book. More complete bibliographies are available by contacting the information centers listed later. As stated earlier, these books may not be available in local libraries or bookstores, although B. Dalton and Barnes and Noble were beginning to add sections on disability issues at the time this list was compiled. If you wish to purchase books, contact a bookstore that places orders regularly with prompt delivery. It may be more expedient to contact the publisher directly. A bookstore or library can provide you with addresses and phone numbers of publishers. You also could contact local parent support groups; some of these groups maintain a library.

For All Disabilities

Callanan, Charles R. *Since Owen.* Baltimore: Johns Hopkins University Press, 1990.
    This lengthy book uses the personal story of the Callanans and their son Owen, who is severely disabled, to open a wealth of information about raising a child with a disability; appendices include extensive resource lists.

Moore, Cory. *A Reader's Guide: For Parents of Children with Mental, Physical, or Emotional Disabilities.* 3rd ed. Rockville, Md.: Woodbine House, 1990.
    This guide is a valuable source of information. It contains annotated bibliographies of books and other literature dealing with many different types of disabilities. In addition, it includes addresses of national organizations, periodicals, and directories. Publishers' addresses and telephone numbers are included in an appendix. It is organized in an easy-to-read format with chapters for specific disabilities and sections titled "Basic Reading," "Your

Child at Home," "Your Child at School," "Your Child Grows Up," "Personal Accounts," and "Where to Write for Information."

Specific Disabilities

Autism

Powers, Michael D., ed. *Children with Autism, A Parent's Guide.* Rockville, Md.: Woodbine House, 1989.

Cerebral Palsy

Schleichkorn, Jay. *Coping with Cerebral Palsy: Answers to Questions Parents Often Ask.* Austin: Pro-Ed, 1983.

Tomlinson, Elaine Geralis, ed. *Children with Cerebral Palsy, A Parent's Guide.* Rockville, Md.: Woodbine House, 1990.

Chronically Ill or Disabled

Jones, Monica Loose. *Home Care for the Chronically Ill or Disabled Child.* New York: Harper and Row, 1985.

Down Syndrome

Pueschel, Siegfried, M.D. *A Parent's Guide to Down Syndrome: Toward a Brighter Future.* Baltimore: Paul H. Brookes, 1990.

Stray-Gunderson, Karen, ed. *Babies with Down Syndrome: A New Parent's Guide.* Rockville, Md.: Woodbine House, 1986.

Dwarfing Conditions

Ablon, Joan. *Little People in America: The Social Dimensions of Dwarfism.* New York: Praeger, 1984.

Van Etton, Angela Muir. *Dwarfs Don't Live in Dollhouses.* Rochester, N.Y.: Adaptive Living, 1988.

Fetal Alcohol Syndrome

Dorris, Michael. *The Broken Cord.* New York: Harper and Row, 1989.

Mental Retardation

Smith, Romayne. *Children with Mental Retardation: A Parent's Guide.* Rockville, Md.: Woodbine House, 1990.

Physical Disabilities

Thompson, Charlotte E., M.D. *Raising a Handicapped Child: A Helpful Guide for Parents of the Physically Disabled.* New York: Ballantine, 1986.

Spina Bifida

Bloom, Beth-Ann, and Seljeskog, Edward. *A Parent's Guide to Spina Bifida.* Minneapolis: University of Minnesota Press, 1988.

Williamson, G. Gordon, ed. *Children with Spina Bifida: Early Intervention and Pre-school Programming.* Baltimore: Paul H. Brookes, 1987.

LOSS, GRIEF, AND ADJUSTMENT

Bozarth-Campbell, Alla. *Life is Goodbye, Life is Hello: Grieving Well through All Kinds of Loss.* Minneapolis: CompCare Publishers, 1986.
   A thorough discussion of grief and symptoms of grief including a chapter on birth and parenting losses, accompanied by poetry.
———. *A Journey through Grief: Gentle, Specific Help to Get You through the Most Difficult Stages of Grieving.* Minneapolis: CompCare Publishers, 1990.
   This short and easy-to-read book offers similar suggestions and some of the same poetry as the book listed above.
Jewett, Claudia L. *Helping Children Cope with Separation and Loss.* Harvard: The Harvard Common Press, 1982.
   Though directed at losses such as death of a close family member or being moved to a new family, the suggestions are helpful for parents of children who "lose" their siblings to adoption.
Kushner, Harold S. *When Bad Things Happen to Good People.* New York: Avon Paperback, 1983.
   Rabbi Kushner's son died of progeria. His book deals with the spiritual issues faced by people who suffer from loss.
Panuthos, Claudia, and Romeo, Catherine. *Ended Beginnings: Healing Childbearing Losses.* New York: Warner Books, 1984.
   It addresses issues surrounding losses due to miscarriage, abortion, adoption, birth defects, stillbirth, and infant death and includes suggestions to help parents begin emotional healing.
Simons, Robin. *After the Tears: Parents Talk about Raising a Child with a Disability.* San Diego: Harcourt, Brace, Jovanovich, 1985.
   The book includes parents' quotes addressing issues about raising a child with a disability, with practical suggestions for coping.
Stearns, Ann Kaiser. *Living through Personal Crisis.* New York: Ballantine, 1984.
   It examines grief and offers suggestions for healing.
Toder, Francine. *When Your Child Is Gone: Learning to Live Again after a Custody Decision, Disappearance, Miscarriage, or Death.* New York: Ballantine, 1986.
   The book includes loss due to adoption, with suggestions for coping with loss.

POETRY ABOUT ADOPTION

Johnston, Patricia, comp. *Perspectives on a Grafted Tree: Thoughts for Those Touched by Adoption.* Indianapolis: Perspectives Press, 1983.
   This collection of poems is written by birthparents, adoptive parents, and adoptees.

PRENATAL TESTING

Blatt, Robin J. R. *Prenatal Tests—What They Are, Their Benefits and Risks, and How to Decide Whether to Have Them or Not.* New York: Vintage, 1988.

This guide for pregnant women and their partners is intended to help them make informed decisions about prenatal care; an updated version was being developed during the writing of this book.

SIBLING/FAMILY RELATIONSHIPS

Cairo, Shelly. *Our Brother Has Down Syndrome.* Toronto: Annick Press, 1985.

Written by sisters of a boy with Down syndrome, this book offers pictures and simple text suitable for children.

Featherstone, Helen. *A Difference in the Family.* New York: Viking Penguin, 1980.

It's an emotional account of relationships in families of children with handicaps.

Kupfer, Fern. *Before and After Zachariah.* Chicago: Academy Chicago Publishers, 1982.

This is a poignant story of the Kupfers' life with their son Zachariah, who is severely disabled and now lives in an institution.

Perske, Robert. *Hope for the Families: New Directions for Parents of Persons with Retardation or Other Disabilities.* Nashville: Abingdon Press, 1987.

It includes illustrations by Martha Perske.

Powell, Thomas H., and Ogle, Peggy Ahrenhold. *Brothers and Sisters—A Special Part of Exceptional Families.* Baltimore: Paul H. Brookes, 1985.

This book discusses the needs of children who have siblings with disabilities.

Trainer, Marilyn. *Differences In Common: Straight Talk on Mental Retardation, Down Syndrome, and Life.* Rockville, Md.: Woodbine, 1991.

A collection of almost fifty essays, this book describes family life with Ben, the Trainers' son who has Down syndrome, from birth through young adulthood.

Turnbull, H. Rutherford, III, and Turnbull, Ann. *Parents Speak Out, Then and Now.* 2nd ed. Columbus: Charles Merrill, 1985.

This collection of stories is written by parents of children with disabilities.

MAGAZINE ARTICLES

Chase, Janet. "Not Quite the Baby I Expected." *Good Housekeeping,* October 1984, 68.

Fein, Elaine. "Should We Keep Our Baby?" *Women's Day,* 20 January 1987, 68.

Finnegan, Joanne. "A Home for Brian." *Parenting,* March 1991, 114–18.

Kupfer, Fern. "Not Home for the Holidays." *Family Circle,* 20 December 1988, 226.

Springen, Karen, and Dantrowitz, Barbara. "The Long Goodbye." *Newsweek,* 22 October 1990, 77–80.

Wooldridge, Randy. "I Couldn't Keep My Baby." *Working Mother,* September 1989, 20–24.

PERIODICALS

The Exceptional Parent
1170 Commonwealth Avenue
Third Floor
Boston, MA 02134
tel. 617-730-5800

Sharing Our Caring
P.O. Box 400
Milton, WA 98354
The articles, written primarily by parents, and pictures are all about children
with Down syndrome.

Special Parent/Special Child
Lindell Press
P.O. Box 462
South Salem, NY 10590
It focuses on helping children with disabilities to learn developmental skills.

NATIONAL ORGANIZATIONS

Disabilities

The following organizations can provide information about disabilities. These
are only suggested and not in any way endorsed by the publisher or author of
this book. If you don't find a particular disability listed, try contacting a large
organization that reaches a more general population (e.g., Association of Retarded Citizens, Association of Birth Defect Children, or National Organization
of Rare Disorders). Also, the larger organizations often will connect you with
local chapters.

These resources were accurate at the time of compilation, but unfortunately,
both phone numbers and addresses often change. Again, the larger federal organizations would be a source for addresses and telephone numbers if the ones
below do not connect you with the organization you wish to reach. Make use of
local resources, such as genetic centers, parent support groups, or your doctors
to help you locate national organizations and support groups. It may take persistence and patience, but there are support and information organizations out
there for parents of children with many different disabilities.

Some of these organizations will be able to provide information about adoption, others won't. Adoption agencies/organizations follow this listing.

Association for Retarded Citizens (ARC)
National Headquarters
500 East Border Street, Suite 300
Arlington, TX 76010
tel. 800-433-5255 or 817-261-6003
(The national headquarters can give you addresses of local branches of ARC.)

Association of Birth Defect Children
5400 Diplomat Circle, Suite 270
Orlando, FL 32810
tel. 407-629-1466

Autism Society of America
8601 Georgia Avenue, Suite 503
Silver Spring, MD 20910
tel. 301-565-0433

Cornelia de Lange Syndrome
60 Dyer Avenue
Collinsville, CT 06022
tel. 800-223-8355 (outside Connecticut) or 203-693-0159

Cystic Fibrosis Foundation
6931 Arlington Road
Bethesda, MD 20814
tel. 800-FIGHT CF or 301-951-4422

Epilepsy Foundation of America
4351 Garden City Drive
Landover, MD 20785
tel. 800-332-1000 or 301-459-3700

Federation for Children with Special Needs
95 Berkeley Street, Suite 104
Boston, MA 02116
tel. 617-482-2915

Fetal Alcohol Network
158 Rosemont Avenue
Coatesville, PA 19320
tel. 215-384-1133

5p– Society (cri du chat)
11609 Oakmont
Overland Park, KS 66210
tel. 913-469-8900

International Rett Syndrome
8511 Rose Marie Drive
Fort Washington, MD 20744
tel. 301-248-7031

I.V.H. Parents (Intraventricular Hemorrhage)
P.O. Box 56-111
Miami, FL 33156
tel. 305-232-0381

Little People of America
P.O. Box 9897
Washington, DC 20016
tel. 301-589-0730

March of Dimes Birth Defects Foundation
1275 Mamaroneck Avenue
White Plains, NY 10605
tel. 914-428-7100

National Down Syndrome Congress
1800 Dempster Street
Park Ridge, IL 60068-1146
tel. 800-232-NDSC (outside Illinois) or 312-823-7550

National Down Syndrome Society
666 Broadway
New York, NY 10012
tel. 800-221-4602 or 212-460-9330

National Easter Seal Society
70 East Lake Street
Chicago, IL 60601
tel. 312-726-6200 (voice), 312-726-4258 (TDD)

National Fragile X Foundation
1441 York Street, Suite 215
Denver, CO 80206
tel. 800-688-8765 or 303-333-6155

National Hemophilia Foundation
The Soho Building
110 Greene Street, Suite 303
New York, NY 10012
tel. 212-219-8180

National Hydrocephalus Foundation
Route 1, River Road
Box 210A
Joliet, IL 60436
tel. 815-467-6548

National Information Center for Children and Youth with
Handicaps (NICHCY)
P.O. Box 1492
Washington, D.C. 20013
tel. 703-893-6061 or 800-999-5599
(The center provides free information to parents of children with handicaps.)

National MPS Society, Inc. (Mucopolysaccharidoses)
17 Kraemer Street
Hicksville, NY 11801
tel. 516-931-6338

National Organization for Rare Disorders, Inc. (NORD)
P.O. Box 8923
New Fairfield, CT 06812-1783
tel. 800-447-6673 or 203-746-6518

National Tay-Sachs and Allied Diseases Association
2001 Beacon Street
Brookline, MA 02146
tel. 617-277-4463

Osteogenesis Imperfecta Foundation, Inc.
P.O. Box 14807
Clearwater, FL 34629-4807
tel. 813-855-7077

Prader-Willi Syndrome Association
6490 Excelsior Boulevard, Suite E-102
St. Louis Park, MN 55426
tel. 612-926-1947

Retinitis Pigmentosa Foundation Fighting Blindness
1401 Mt. Royal Avenue
Baltimore, MD 21217
tel. 800-638-2300 or 301-225-9400
(The foundation also offers information for parents of children with Laurence-Moons-Bardet-Biedl Syndrome.)

Sibling Information Network
Connecticut's University Affiliated Program on
Developmental Disabilities
991 Main Street, Suite 3A
East Hartford, CT 06108
tel. 203-282-7050

Siblings for Significant Change
105 East 22nd Street
New York, NY 10010
tel. 212-420-0776

S.O.F.T. (Support Organization for Trisomy 18/13)
c/o Barbara VanHerreweghe
2982 Union Street
Rochester, NY 14624
tel. 716-594-4621

Spina Bifida Association of America
4590 MacArthur Blvd.
Suite 250
Washington, D.C. 20007
tel. 800-621-3141 or 301-770-SBAA

TASH: The Association for Persons with Severe Handicaps
11201 Greenwood Avenue North
Seattle, WA 98133
tel. 206-361-8870

Turner Syndrome Society of the United States
768-214 Twelve Oaks Center

15500 Wayzata Boulevard
Wayzata, MN 55391
tel. 612-475-9944

UCP National Office of New York (Cerebral Palsy)
7 Penn Plaza, Suite 804
New York, NY 10001
tel. 212-268-6655

U.S. Department of Health and Human Services Public Health Service/National Institute of Neurological and Communicative Disorders and Stroke/National Institutes of Health
9000 Rockville Pike
Bethesda, MD 20892
tel. 301-496-4000
(The department offers the *Hope through Research* series with the following titles: *Autism, Cerebral Palsy, Epilepsy, Hearing Loss, Spina Bifida,* and *Tourette Syndrome.*)

Adoption

The following organizations may provide information that will connect you with local adoption agencies that handle special needs adoptions. Most act only as referrals or match adoptive and birth families. A local agency or lawyer usually will be necessary to complete an adoption plan.

AASK (Adopt a Special Kid)
3530 Grand Avenue
Oakland, CA 94610
tel. 415-451-1748

AASK Midwest (Adopt a Special Kid)
1605 Holland Road, Suite A-5
Maumee, OH 43537
tel. 419-891-0327

Adoption of Children with Spina Bifida
1955 Florida Drive
Xenia, OH 45385
tel. 513-372-2040

Adoption Options
2332 Eastgate, Suite B
Baton Rouge, LA 70816
tel. 504-291-4588 or 504-647-3179

National Down Syndrome Adoption Exchange
56 Midchester Avenue
White Plains, NY 10606
tel. 914-428-1236

National Resource Center for Special Needs Adoption
17390 West Eight Mile Road
Southfield, MI 48075
tel. 313-443-0300

North American Council on Adoptable Children
1821 University Avenue, Suite N498
St. Paul, MN 55104
tel. 612-644-3036

Project Impact
25 West Street
Boston, MA 02111
tel. 617-451-1472

Index

About the Author

JOANNE FINNEGAN is a high school mathematics teacher who, because of her personal experience with a child born with Down syndrome, has written articles for magazines and journals about adoption of children with special needs. She speaks to medical groups about the adoption option, and actively participates in a nationwide telephone support network for parents who are considering this option.